SOCIAL CONSTRUCT

Social Constructionisms

Approaches to the Study of the Human World

By

Titus Hjelm

First published 2014 by
PALGRAVE MACMILLAN

Palgrave Macmillan in the UK is an imprint of Macmillan Publishers Limited,
registered in England, company number 785998, of Houndmills, Basingstoke,
Hampshire RG21 6XS.

Palgrave Macmillan in the US is a division of St Martin's Press LLC,
175 Fifth Avenue, New York, NY 10010.

Palgrave Macmillan is the global academic imprint of the above companies
and has companies and representatives throughout the world.

Palgrave® and Macmillan® are registered trademarks in the United States,
the United Kingdom, Europe and other countries

ISBN: 978-1-4039-3999-9 hardback
ISBN: 978-1-4039-4000-1 paperback

This book is printed on paper suitable for recycling and made from fully
managed and sustained forest sources. Logging, pulping and manufacturing
processes are expected to conform to the environmental regulations of the
country of origin.

A catalogue record for this book is available from the British Library.

A catalog record for this book is available from the Library of Congress.

Typeset by Cambrian Typesetters, Camberley, Surrey

Printed in China

To the memory of Kaarina Hjelm, who was there in the beginning
and
to Lempi Hjelm, who, I hope, will be there in the end.

Contents

List of Tables and Figure

Preface and Acknowledgements

I missed the deadline for this book so many times that it is safe to say that I have been thinking about writing it for most of my academic career. The manuscript, in its various stages, has travelled with me not only in time, but through three different universities and three different countries. But, thinking about writing is, of course, one thing and actually writing, another. I am convinced, however, that the more grey hairs my constant delays caused my patient publisher, the more mature is the end result.

Let me tell you why.

More than ten years ago, as a newish PhD student, I experienced one of those revelations that one sometimes has in academia – the feeling that an idea or theory sums up what you have been thinking about for some time already. Social constructionism was that idea (if not a 'theory' in a strict sense) for me. Like all recent converts, I read and appropriated constructionist ideas with little critical engagement, although I was starting to discern differences within the field. It was a footnote and a random encounter that started the journey, the end result which is the book you are holding. A footnote in a Finnish textbook on discourse analysis (Suoninen, 1999: 35) encouraged me to think about a book which would focus on the internal differences within social constructionism and the usefulness of 'constructionism' as an umbrella term in the first place. Meeting literary agent Jo Campling at a seminar organized by the Finnish Literature Society encouraged me to put my thoughts on paper in proposal form. And here we are.

My thinking about social constructionism has changed with the times. When I first presented the proposal to Jo, not only was constructionism all the rage in the social sciences, but also something that I personally saw as the most revelatory and liberating perspective on scholarship. Now, of course, constructionism is discussed in less unambiguously positive terms. As everyone who knows my taste in music can tell, I've never followed fashion, but I have also come to think of constructionism in more critical and detached terms in recent years. For fashion, I should probably call myself a 'critical realist' – not that being fashionable necessarily makes an approach less worthy – but I like the good old label of constructionist still, even if perhaps a 'critical constructionist'. In this book my point has not been to take a strong position regarding the different traditions of constructionism, but you can probably read this critical perspective between the lines.

Having time to read and learn more is one reason my thinking has evolved. Having had a chance to meet many new and brilliant colleagues during the years is another. Of these, my friends in Helsinki, Amsterdam and London have all had a major impact on my thinking and the overall way I have experienced academic life – not to mention the often more fleeting but profound friendships made through international scholarly networks. I am in the happy situation where mentioning all these people would take too many pages, so I'll settle for mentioning those who had a direct impact on the book: Jim Beckford, Steven Engler, Elisa Heinämäki, Richard Mole, Atte Oksanen and Jim Spickard read parts or the whole manuscript and gave priceless advice. The usual caveat about the remaining faults being mine applies. I would also like to thank the publisher's three anonymous reviewers for helpful comments. It was with great sadness that I learned that Jo Campling, who took me under her wing and got me a contract before I had even finished my PhD, passed away during the writing of the book. Needless to say, I owe her enormously for her trust and open-mindedness. Embarrassingly, the list of people that I've worked with at Palgrave – some of who have already moved on – is also too long to be included here. For their patience, a humble thank you to Steven Kennedy, Lloyd Langman, Anna Reeve, Emily Salz and Beverley Tarquini.

Finally, Nora Kajantie shared the writing of the book – more often the stresses than the triumphs – with me. Not only did she give me her support during the years, but also the world's most beautiful daughter, Lempi. Love is a social construction, but it is a very real one.

The author and publisher would like to thank Blackwell Publishing Ltd. for permission to reproduce an adapted version of 'Table 9.1 Theories of moral panics: motives and origin' from *Moral Panics: The Social Construction of Deviance* (1994) by E. Goode and N. Ben-Yehuda.

The World We Make: The Idea of Social Construction

1

My alarm clock goes off at seven on a normal weekday morning. I get up –
more often than not sleepy and grumpy – and go to the kitchen to put on a
kettle for tea. I make breakfast for my daughter and myself, drink my tea, and
check the morning headlines in the news, or read a book. After that I take a
shower, shave, brush my teeth, comb my hair, put on my clothes, dress my
daughter, and take her to the nursery. Arriving at work, I greet the receptionist in the lobby and answer 'Fine thank you, and you?' to a 'How are you?'
question asked by a colleague in the school lift. I drop my bag at the office and
pop into the men's toilet before the first lecture starts. Entering the classroom,
I say 'Good morning, everyone. Today we are going to discuss social constructionism.'

I won't bore you with the rest of the day, but that is a quite accurate
description of an average morning in my life. Now, I would like you to write
down your average morning routine. After that, let's take a look at an alternative version of my morning.

I wake up to sounds coming from my daughter's room. The sun is shining.
I make breakfast for my daughter and myself and complain about the coming
day to an uninterested toddler. I put on yesterday's slightly smelly clothes. On
the other hand, without showering and brushing my teeth I'll smell anyway.
My chin is stubbly and my hair tangled, but who cares? I take my daughter to
the nursery, and complain about the coming day to the staff. Arriving at work
I let out an audible 'hmph' to the greetings of the receptionist. A colleague in
the lift greets me with a 'How are you?'; I respond by telling him that I think
I have cancer. After dropping my bag I pop into the women's toilet, to the horror of another colleague. Entering the classroom, I say 'Alright folks, another
day at the grind – except today we're going to sit in class naked.' Many of the
students smile in confusion at first, but are soon packing their things when I
start to take off my trousers.[1]

If, while reading the above, you thought that the reactions of my colleagues
and students were justified, I don't blame you. So do I. My imagined actions
would be considered as impolite, potentially as harassment, and most likely

the actions of a mentally disturbed person. If you look at your own morning routine it probably resembles my first example more than the second. I am not surprised. It is *common sense* to act as I did in the first example.

Yet, if we look at the individual actions in the examples more closely, there is nothing 'natural' or inevitable about them. Why should we get up for work or school at times when it's pitch dark outside and we could easily sleep a couple of more hours? Why are we expected to take care of our personal hygiene? Sure, we'll have more cavities without dental care, but why should we shave or spend time fixing our hair? And if you're asked 'How are you?', shouldn't you reply with whatever your current assessment of your physical and mental state is? Toilets have the same function, no matter what the symbol on the door. Finally, providing the heating works, why shouldn't people sit in class naked?

Just asking these questions feels absurd, because all these things are so ingrained in our modern way of life. Some more so than others: It takes time for some people from non-Anglo-American cultures to understand that more often than not 'How are you?' is just a different version of 'hello' rather than a serious enquiry into one's wellbeing. Yet, perhaps with the exception of some tribal people unaffected by Western norms of covering the body, most people would shrink back from nudity in the workplace. The point here is that doing the above things 'right' is a matter of *convention*, where the correct way of acting in a situation is imposed or agreed upon at some point and has become so commonplace that it has become taken for granted. These conventions that become habits make social life as we know it possible, so they're never 'just' conventions. But the important point is that a convention created by people can also be changed by people. Social constructionism argues that the human world is not as simple and obvious as it seems and that people, you and I, take actively part in producing and reproducing – constructing – it.[2]

The challenge of social constructionism: rethinking the human world

The idea that the world as we know it is a 'social construction', a product of human interaction, has become a central metaphor in social science (Restivo and Croissant, 2008: 220; Elder-Vass, 2012: i) – a key framework for examining society and culture. Although I keep referring to the more familiar terms 'society' and 'culture', the term 'human world' nicely captures what I think of as the subject matter of this book: it is 'the aspect of the world, that bears the imprint of human activity, that would not exist at all but for the actions of human beings' (Bauman, 1990: 3, quoted in Jenkins, 2002: 3). In this human world, what we take for granted, as 'common sense', is not as simple as we have thought. What seem to be unquestioned ways of doing things turn out to be conventions, habits, and agreements. What we have forgotten during history is that there would be no social life without people, and that people came up with the conventions, habits and agreements in the first place. Social constructionism draws attention to this and the idea that if and when the social reality we experience every day is a human construction, it can also be changed by human action. Our destiny is affected, but not defined, by biological or psychological characteristics, nor by the way society is structured.

This book aims to chart the different ways the idea of social construction has been employed in the social sciences. It focuses on the sociological contributions to constructionist discussions, but also tackles ideas in constructionist social psychology. The argument running through the text is simple: there is no one 'constructionism' (or 'constructivism', see below) we can point to, but rather many constructionisms – as the title of the book implies. These different constructionist traditions or perspectives sensitize us to different aspects of social and cultural life and come with particular assumptions about how we can know about the human world and how best to study it social-scientifically. Although the diversity of traditions and the consequences of this diversity are the gist of the book, it makes sense to begin with some general characteristics that traditions claiming to be 'constructionist' almost always share.

In the first place, understanding social constructionism requires what could be described as an inverse suspension of disbelief. 'Suspension of disbelief' is a literary term that, according to the *Oxford English Dictionary* refers to the 'voluntary withholding of scepticism on the part of the reader with regard to incredible characters and events'. In other words, it doesn't matter that we know that Frodo, Gandalf, and Sauron are fictional characters, because there are important thoughts, ideas and human interests conveyed in an 'unrealistic' fantasy story like Tolkien's *The Lord of the Rings*. Social constructionism invites us to do the same to our everyday lives, by showing that what we consider as unproblematically 'real' is actually contingent on what we think and do. Unicorns will not exist just because we would like them to, but by thinking about and communicating about a different way of understanding the role of women in the world, for example, we can change things. *Contingency*, therefore, is a key term in understanding social constructionism. Things and ideas in the human world – the world that would not exist without the humans in it – are not inevitable, but products of human action.

This revelation, if you will, has had the consequence that much of constructionist research has played a *liberating* role in at least two senses. First, it has showed how ideas about motherhood, for example, are products of historical and social processes:

> Mothers who accept current canons of emotion and behavior may learn that the ways they are supposed to feel are not ordained by human nature or the biology of reproduction. They need not feel quite as guilty as they are supposed to, if they do not obey either the old rules of family or whatever is the official psycho-pediatric rule of the day (Hacking, 1999: 2).

Although constructionist analyses of various topics have showed their liberating potential, Hacking (1999: 2) goes on to say that sometimes talk of 'construction' can be of little help to those whose problems are being constructed, like in the case of anorexia. Second, constructionism has been considered liberating in the sense that 'social constructionist movements have tended to emerge as self-consciously critical of the institutional mainstream of the various academic disciplines within which they are found' (Weinberg, 2008: 15). The following chapters show that this has been more or less the case for all of the traditions discussed in this book. Constructionism has emerged from the questioning of the paradigmatic ways of thinking about the central questions and methods of a discipline. Different constructionisms combine the two senses of liberation and critique in different portions, but it is safe to say that one or the other is present in all types.

As a result of the focus on contingency and liberation, constructionists pay careful attention to the *social processes* in which the human world is constructed (Burr, 1995: 4; Hacking, 1999: 49). I will return to the issue of what kind of questions constructionist research is best fit to answer in Chapter 7, but suffice it to say here that the idea of process assumes that the construction of ideas, for example, takes place in stages in history. Hence, constructionist enquiry is always sensitive to issues of *historicity*, which in this context means more than 'it actually happened' – rather that ideas do not pop up from nowhere, but are products of people's thinking and communicating in a sequence of time.

If contingency, process and liberation could be called the shared 'characteristics' of constructionism, there are also four 'functions' that follow from these characteristics: (1) constructionism offers a view of what the human world is like, what it consists of (the *ontological* function); (2) it offers a view of how knowledge of the human world is produced (the *epistemological* function); and (3) it argues that (1) and (2) make it possible for people to change the human world by thinking and communicating differently about it (the *critical*

Table 1.1   The characteristics and functions of constructionisms

Characteristics

1. Contingency	The human world is a human product
2. Liberation	Categories and definitions can be changed
3. Process	Construction is an interactive and historical achievement

Functions

1. Ontological	What the human world consists of
2. Epistemological	How knowledge of the human world is produced
3. Critical	How to change the human world by thinking and communicating differently
4. Methodological	How to study the processes of construction

function). The chapters that follow demonstrate how these functions are combined, if at all, in different constructionist traditions. In addition, there is a fourth function, which examines the best way to study the processes of construction (the *methodological* function). The key term here is discourse, which warrants a more in-depth discussion because it also illuminates the abovementioned core aspects of constructionism.

Text and talk as doing: the centrality of discourse

Constructionists are divided over what it is exactly that is doing the construction. Knowledge, culture, language and discourse have all been offered as choices (for a comprehensive discussion, see Elder-Vass, 2012). While there are good grounds to favour any of the above, I have opted for discourse, which – I think – best captures what is going on when something is said to be socially constructed.

The concept of 'discourse' entered the humanities and social sciences in the 1970s and gained increasing popularity with the advent of poststructuralism and postmodernism in the 1980s, so much so that is justified to speak of a 'discursive turn'. Crucial to this development was the work of Michel Foucault (especially 1978; 1995), who argued that discourse was the defining aspect of social relations and, consequently, saw the study of discourse as central to the study of how individuals ('subjects') and society are constituted discursively, that is, in practical *language use* by people who interact with other people.[3] Discourse theory and analysis has diversified since, and there are few definitions of 'discourse' that catch a meaning that is shared by all who use the concept. What *is* shared by all of the approaches is a commitment to at least some of the principles of social constructionism outlined above.

Although 'discourse' often pops up in discussions of 'discourse analysis', this has 'the unfortunate consequence that it is sometimes treated as a method only, a technique something on a par with an experiment or a questionnaire' (Edwards and Potter, 1992: 11), whereas actually 'there is more than a methodological shift at work; there is some fairly radical theoretical rethinking' (Edwards and Potter, 1992: 11; see also Mills, 2004: 117; Bloor and Wood, 2006: 54). The first aspect of this theoretical rethinking is that discourse is considered *constitutive*, because it does not simply reflect or represent things 'out there' in the world (or in an individual's mind) but 'constitutes' – constructs – them (Fairclough, 1992: 3). Our descriptions of the world are by definition incomplete: while we might be telling the truth and nothing but the truth, we can never tell the *whole* truth about the world (see Barker, 2011: 200). Our discourse is therefore always partial – both in the sense of incomplete and biased – and constructs the world from a particular point of view. When a divorced couple battles over the custody of children in a court, they are both describing the same family, but very likely in quite different ways.

The constitutive aspect is closely linked to the second aspect of discourse, its 'action orientation', that is, how things are *done* with discourse (Edwards and Potter, 1992: 2–3; see Potter and Wetherell, 1987: 32–3; Potter, 1996: 105). For example, the sentence 'it is going to drive me mad doing all those statistics by hand tonight' can be read as a simple announcement. However, if uttered in the presence of a friend in possession of a calculator, its potential meaning changes into a veiled question (Potter and Wetherell, 1987: 33). Because of the action orientation of discourse, analysing processes of social construction is never about analysing text and talk *as such*. Although I don't want to anticipate the methodological discussion in Chapter 7 too much at this point, it is good to mention here that *what is said* is the first, descriptive, step in constructionist analyses. Discourse should, however, be understood as a *social practice*, which in turn means that the second step is to examine *what is done* with discourse. Texts and talk conceptualized as doing goes to the very heart of social constructionist thinking.

Constructionism or constructivism?

If you have come across the idea of social construction before, there is a good chance that you have been reading or hearing about 'social constructionism', 'social constructivism', or perhaps just 'constructionism' and 'constructivism'. On some levels the difference is unproblematic – certainly the terms are often used interchangeably. But there are several reasons why I prefer 'social constructionism'. First, the 'social' in constructionism is sometimes thought of as redundant, because the way 'construction' is used always refers to processes of social interaction. The 'social' remains, however, a useful reminder that even when we are constructing ideas about the world, say, by watching television, there is always a human producer to the programme, and that makes the idea of construction broader than an analysis of individual 'readings' of, say, television programmes. However, I will for the sake of brevity often refer to just 'constructionism' on the following pages, assuming that the title of the book will remind the reader of the 'social' aspects of construction processes. Second, although perhaps more often than not '(social) constructivism' is used to refer to the very same thing as '(social) constructionism', in some cases there is marked difference between the two. In educational psychology, for example, construct*ivism* refers to a theory of learning that posits that knowledge is constructed in the individual's mind and is a cognitive function, whereas construct*ionism* is based on a critique of this very idea, instead arguing that knowledge construction is a process of social interaction. Consequently, cognition features little in constructionism, where the focus is on language and interaction (Gergen and Wortham, 2001: 121–24; Holstein and Gubrium, 2008: 8). Likewise, Barbara Herrnstein Smith (2006: 5) proposes that whereas 'constructivism' is concerned with 'dynamics and processes of cognition', 'social constructionism' is 'more culturally focused and politically engaged' – thus adding the critical function to constructionism.

Keeping the 'social' in constructionism as a reminder of the importance of interaction and making a difference between perspectives based on interaction and cognitive theories of knowledge formation are the minimal housekeeping rules that I want to impose in this book. Other than that, it is important to acknowledge that after almost 50 years of usage, the term 'social construction-ism' and its derivatives are empty in themselves – which is also the claim of critical approaches that (quite rightly) argue that saying that something is 'socially constructed' has become a tag which is often inadequately explained or examined in research purporting to be constructionist. That is why the dili-gent student of constructionism must always ask *what kind* of construction-ism is an article, book, or presentation talking about; what traditions of social constructionism are discussed. The rest of the book offers guidelines for exact-ly that.

The four traditions: plan of the book

This book is organized around different traditions of social constructionism. Thus, Chapter 2 discusses a strand of sociological constructionism associated with Peter L. Berger and Thomas Luckmann and their field-defining book *The Social Construction of Reality* (1966). Chapter 3 examines the constructionist approach to social problems research. Chapter 4 explores constructionist ideas in (social) psychology, and its links to postmodern thought. Chapter 5 is a dis-cussion of critical discourse analysis, especially in the work of Norman Fairclough, a pioneer of the field. While somewhat idiosyncratic – as any choice of traditions in a field that is in constant flux – the choice of traditions is representative of the diversity of approaches that constitutes the field. Other authors (for example, Potter, 1996; Payne, 1999) represent the central tradi-tions differently, but in the context of this book the point is less to give an authoritative genealogy of the term than to explore the most distinct tradi-tions.

It would have made as much sense to structure the chapters based on the key characteristics of constructionist thinking, like some others have done (for example, Burr, 1995; 2003), but the focus on traditions highlights the main point that I want to make: It makes little sense to talk about 'social construc-tionism' as a monolithic whole. There are rather different currents in a wide stream that, while sharing some aspects, are quite different in other aspects. Holstein and Gubrium (2008: 3) call this the constructionist 'mosaic'. The four perspectives in this book represent what I think are some of the main cur-rents, also demonstrating that, ultimately, instead of 'social constructionism' it would be more helpful to talk about social constructionisms in the plural. If there is one thing I would like the reader to take home after reading the book, it is this.

Structuring the book by traditions is, I think, justified by the field of constructionism itself. With the important exception of Holstein and Gubrium's comprehensive *Handbook of Constructionist Research* (2008), there is little overlap between the traditions. Thus, the sociological constructionism of Berger and Luckmann gets a ritual mention in many works, but is engaged directly by only few. There is almost no cross-pollination between constructionist approaches to social problems and discursive social psychology, and while discursive social psychology and critical discourse analysis spring from similar backgrounds, their take on the role of discourse vis-à-vis the world outside discourse is markedly different. Acknowledging this, I will present the traditions relatively independently and will examine the similarities and differences in Chapter 6. Chapter 6 also discusses criticisms of constructionism. Chapter 7 then closes by examining how constructionist ideas can be put into practical use in social-scientific research, and what tools constructionism can offer us for participation in civil society.

The danger with this approach is, of course, that the internal diversity of the traditions is misrepresented. For example, certainly not all of discursive social psychology is 'postmodern' in any meaningful sense. Also, as I note below, not everyone would automatically associate critical discourse analysis with constructionism in the first place. Alas, this is a necessary evil in a work like this and I have tried to tackle questions of how representative my take on a tradition is whenever they arise. Finally, I have not tried to hide my personal preferences. Coming from a particular tradition of social science myself, I have not found all of the perspectives discussed here equally feasible. I have nevertheless tried to maintain a spirit of *dialogue* where the reality of social constructionism itself is constantly in motion – as it should be.

Case studies: Satanism scares and scientific revolutions

Throughout the book I will illustrate the theoretical ideas and questions raised in the chapters with case studies that apply the particular tradition of constructionism to everyday life. I will begin with two cases that are at different levels of abstraction – one that could potentially affect any television viewer, the other a matter of intellectual history – but which nevertheless both illuminate the ways in which constructionism questions our taken for granted ways of looking at the human world.

Satan at the Prom

The Satanism scare gripped the United States and Western Europe from the mid 1980s to the beginning of the new millennium. At the heart of the scare was a belief in an organized and widely spread cult of Satan worshippers, who supposedly committed unspeakable deeds in the name of their infernal master.

A quote from the later-notorious (Bromley, 1991: 63) US talk show, the *Geraldo Show*, sums up the main elements of the phenomenon:

> Estimates are that there are over one million Satanists in this country. The majority of them are linked in a highly organized, very secret network. From small towns to large cities, they have attracted police and FBI attention to their satanic ritual abuse, child pornography, and grisly satanic murders. The odds are that this is happening in your town (*Geraldo Show*, 19 November 1987, quoted in Victor, 1989: 28).

By the end of the 1980s many areas of the United States, from Wisconsin to Louisiana and California to Maine, were afflicted by rumours of a satanic cult threatening the wellbeing of communities, especially children and adolescents. While the claims made in media such as the *Geraldo Show* might seem far-fetched at first sight, they were probably inspired by real feelings of danger in local communities. The Satanism scare, is, on the one hand, an example of social anxiety that was based on very little, if any, empirical evidence. On the other hand, it clearly illustrates how even imaginary beliefs have very real consequences, thus blurring the line between 'hard facts' and doubtful claims. A 'rumour-panic' from rural Pennsylvania, described by folklorist Bill Ellis (1990) is a case in point.

The Prom Night is an American cultural symbol that is well known outside of the United States, thanks to a myriad of portrayals in popular film and literature. The vampire Edward taking his girlfriend Bella to the Prom in *Twilight* is just the latest addition to a long line of Prom representations, most famous of which is probably – and would certainly have been in the late 1980s – the film adaptation of Stephen King's *Carrie*, with its iconic shot of Sissy Spacek bathed in pig's blood (Ellis, 1990: 45). Although the experience of Prom Night is more complex for modern youth than popular culture depictions usually allow (Best, 2000), it still remains an important adolescent experience for many Americans. Without doubt, the Prom is an important nexus of 'school, commercial, and youth cultures [...] wherein kids work through central issues surrounding questions of authority, class, diversity, sexuality, and romance' (Best, 2000: 3). Many anxieties regarding these issues – for students, parents, and educators alike – concentrate around Prom Night, making it an 'exciting' event in more than the Edward and Bella sense.

An example where the idyllic vision of the Prom Night was severely breached happened in rural Pennsylvania in 1987. Towards the end of May a rumour started to circulate among the students of Panther Valley High School in Lansford, Pennsylvania, that a satanic cult active in the area was going to murder some Prom attendants. As Ellis vividly describes, the rumour had multiple variants:

> One type held that 'there was to be three suicides and three murders that night... The first six people in the door would be the six to die.' Another

common version held that the first four couples to arrive would die; or perhaps it would be the first five persons to leave. Others specified that girls wearing a given color dress (usually pink) would be the first to die. How? Some sources thought that the satanists would allegedly either open fire during the 'King and Queen Dance', the dance following the election and coronation of the lucky people; others speculated that the refreshments would be laced with drugs and poison; still others thought that people would be stabbed at the tables, or shot in the parking lot as they left (Ellis, 1990: 27).

The rumours soon escalated and spread to nearby areas. Concerned parents started contacting school authorities and the police. The prom was held, with metal detectors installed at the door of the Prom venue, undercover agents mingling with the students, and police cars cruising the roads outside. Despite the very real concern, 'no fatalities were recorded', as Ellis (1990: 28) dryly notes. None of the rumours turned out to be true. Yet, law enforcement was mobilized, parents worried, and some students missed the prom because of anxieties over satanic killers. How was it possible that apparently unfounded rumours had, nevertheless, very real consequences?

This is what W.I. Thomas, in one of sociology's classic coinages, called the 'definition of the situation'. Thomas's argument was that 'if men [sic] define situations as real, they are real in their consequences' (S. Scott, 2006: 51). What made the seemingly bizarre rumours warranted in the Panther Valley case was, Ellis argues, the religious conservatism of the community and some teenagers' adoption of supposedly 'satanic' symbolism as a vehicle for rebellion. Also, the 'trigger moment' for community anxieties was the unexplained suicide of a popular student (Ellis, 1990: 33).

Research shows that Americans consistently show higher levels of belief in God, Satan, heaven and hell than their European counterparts. This is especially so in (semi-)rural America. If Lansford, Pennsylvania in the 1980s was representative of the average – and there is good reason to believe it was – most of its residents, adults and teens alike, believed that the devil actively causes evil in the world. If that is so, it is only logical that there are people who worship Satan, just as good Christians worship God, and that these devil-worshippers are there to cause harm to good Christians. The last point is important: although I might be tempted to dismiss the beliefs and events around Prom Night in Panther Valley High as 'irrational', even 'delusional', they make sense in the framework of beliefs that the population subscribes to.

These beliefs also seemed to be warranted by some of the local teens who dressed in T-shirts bearing logos and pictures of famous heavy metal artists – at the time Ozzy Osbourne and Mötley Crüe were on top of the 'satanic' metal artist list – and drew '666' (the biblical 'number of the beast') and pentagram (a 'satanic' symbol) graffiti on walls. Some of these teens stole a lamb from a meat-packing plant and slaughtered it. Although this turned out to be a drunken prank, it fuelled the flames of Satanist conspiracy.

Similar 'rebellious' teens – 'weirdos' in the local parlance – were also connected to the suicide of a popular Panther Valley senior. The student came home from a drinking night with friends and, after being confronted by his mother about his drinking, fetched a gun and shot himself in front of his mother (Ellis, 1990: 42). The student hadn't exhibited any signs of depression or suicidal tendencies, so the death didn't make any sense to his friends and co-students, causing wide anxiety. It wasn't long, then, that a rumour started circulating about a suicide cult which the student supposedly belonged to. Unidentified people made threat calls to other students and school personnel, the gravestone of the student was vandalized, and the friends of the dead student beat up some of the 'weirdos'. Again, an unfounded idea about a suicide pact[4] had very real consequences. But 'since the "weirdo" groups could not have been involved in any pact with the dead student, there was no real point in blaming them for the suicide' (Ellis, 1990: 45). The anxieties remained.

The suicide and the suicide cult story resurfaced as an explanation for the Prom Night fears later in the year. Supposedly, the dead student was one of five that made a suicide pact, but since the other four backed out, the 'cult' they belonged to 'threatened to kill someone in area schools before each prom that year' (Ellis, 1990: 43). When this didn't happen, the fears dissipated and the suicide and satanic cults were relegated to memory. Life could go on. As Ellis concludes, the Prom Night might have been a 'delusion', but 'it was on some level a therapeutic one' (Ellis, 1990: 49).

The Satanism scare phenomenon has subsequently spread in some form in many European countries and, most recently, into North Africa and the Middle East (LeVine, 2008). Even in countries where belief in God or the devil is much less common than in the United States, a Satanism scare can develop if the mainstream media uses 'experts' from evangelical backgrounds as information sources, as happened in the Nordic countries, for example (Hjelm et al., 2009). Indeed, if there is one thing that is common to Satanism scares, it is the prevalence of ideas about 'satanic cults' that originate in American Evangelical Christianity and are spread across religious networks worldwide.

The point, again, is that whatever people define as real, becomes real in consequences, regardless of 'objective' reality. Massive resources have been spent in families, education, media, law enforcement and other spheres of society to counter a 'satanic' threat which, at best, has little or no actual foundation or, at worst, becomes a self-fulfilling prophecy when some people decide to adopt satanic symbolism and engage in vandalism or violence to provoke the panic atmosphere. The panic at the Prom shows how everyday 'facts' are socially constructed.

The culture of science

The history of human civilization is often represented as a story of great men – and sometimes, of great women. Turning points in history are personified in characters such as Alexander the Great, the prophet Mohammed, Genghis

Khan, Christopher Columbus, Elizabeth I, Napoleon, Josef Stalin, and George W. Bush. From the history of painting and music we recognize revered names such as Michelangelo, Rembrandt, van Gogh, Picasso, Kahlo, Bach, Beethoven, and Mozart, even if we're not aware of the different schools of painting or composing the belong to. Literature is known for its Austens, Dostoyevskys, and Twains rather than the literary styles they represent. Similar lists could be made of most walks of life from architecture to zoology. The biographies of great individuals are the building blocks of our history.

The history of science is no different in this sense. The image of Galileo lonely up in his observatory, observing the movement of the stars with his telescope, is a familiar one. More recently, Albert Einstein's contributions to western culture have spanned beyond the theory of mass–energy equivalence ($E = mc^2$). The very name 'Einstein' has become a colloquial term for a genius – both in serious and ironic senses – and the famous photo of Einstein sticking out his tongue from 1951 has become an iconic expression of the 'mad scientist'. Contemporary movers and shakers in the world of science may be less familiar to the general public, but famous institutions such as the Nobel Prize nourish the image of science as the achievement of extraordinary individuals making extraordinary discoveries that change our view of the world.

For a long time mainstream philosophy of science supported the received image of the lonely genius because scientific knowledge was given a privileged status compared to 'everyday' knowledge. Unlike everyday knowledge, scientific knowledge was seen by some as free of the 'clutter' of routine thinking and foremost as a logical endeavour, devoid of feeling and subjective preferences. Philosophical accounts were focused on the logic of scientific 'truth' and on the analysis of the concept of experience, creating formal laws that, however, often had little to do with the actual practice of science.

This kind of received view of scientific discovery personified in great individuals and backed by the contemporary view of the philosophy of science received a critical blow in 1962 with the publication of Thomas Kuhn's *The Structure of Scientific Revolutions* (Kuhn, 1996 [1962]). The book became a best-seller, and was at one time the most frequently cited book in the English language (Gergen and Gergen, 2003: 2). Although some of Kuhn's arguments had been explored by earlier historians and philosophers, the book sparked a debate that goes on today and in many ways changed the way we think about scientific discovery.[5]

At the core of Kuhn's argument is the proposition that the practice of science is very much a human endeavour, where interpretations of physical phenomena and theories are formulated in an internal dialogue between practitioners and schools of thought. Every scientist builds upon previous knowledge and is therefore inseparably part of a scientific community. The shared knowledge within the community provides the scientist with concepts and frameworks of thinking. As Kuhn shows, when the achievements of the lonely geniuses are analysed in the context of their contemporary scientific community, a completely different picture from the conventional history of science begins to emerge. Copernicus might be best known to posterity for his ground-breaking ideas on the movement of planets, but at the time he was observing the planets within a commonly shared theory – which later became problematic partly through his own work (Kuhn, 1996: 68–9). In other words, for Kuhn, culture is not just a backcloth for the practice of science; *science is culture* (Barnes, 1982: 10). Scientific knowledge is an achievement of a scientific community in which people form concepts and theories that are dependent on symbolic forms (language, numbers, etc.) produced by the community. The revolutionary part of Kuhn's argument was that scientists can never stand outside this community and observe the world independent of the concepts and theories of the culture of science—a thought that ran against the image of the lonely genius in the history of science and the formulations of science as a strictly logical process in the philosophy of science.

The Structure of Scientific Revolutions brought several new concepts into the discourse of history and philosophy of science, the most famous of which is that of *paradigm*.[6] A paradigm is a consensus about the scientific achievements and problem-solving methods in a particular (natural) science[7] and 'the culture of an established natural science is passed on in the form of paradigms' (Barnes, 1982: 18). Paradigms are most evident in textbooks, which are the main vehicle for passing on the culture of a science. A biology textbook, for example, tells the student not only that biology is the study of living organisms, but also what questions are relevant for the study of biology and what methods are used in trying to answer those questions. The student is socialized into a community of biologists and the prevailing paradigm(s) in biology through lectures and textbook examples. A paradigm therefore creates a mindset of doing things right – an orthodoxy – that is based on socially reinforced practices (see Bird, 2000: 66; Fuller, 1998: 93).

It should be noted that the social sciences are quite different from the natural sciences in the sense that reading a sociology textbook, for example, won't tell the student *the* right way of practicing sociology. Instead, it will show a selection of competing theories, many of which might be old, but which are still actively used in new forms. Individual sociologists might have their own favourite leanings (hence this book on social constructionism!), but few would try to claim that there is only one valid way of practicing sociology. At times strong schools of sociological thinking might dominate – often within a particular national framework – but the alternatives to dominant theories are always visibly present. In the natural sciences theories become obsolete when paradigms change, whereas in the social sciences theories may go out of fashion, only to be revived later.

One of Kuhn's main aims in *The Structure of Scientific Revolutions* was to show that earlier history of science had mistreated now obsolete theories in the sense that their validity was read against the background of what we now know. In addition to debunking the lonely scientist myth, Kuhn's main historical critique was aimed at so-called 'Whig history', which saw history as progress towards the present:

> Rather than seeking the permanent contributions of an older science to our present vantage, [some historians of science] attempt to display the historical integrity of that science in its own time. They ask, for example, not about the relation of Galileo's views to those of modern science, but rather about the relationship between his views and those of his group, i.e., his teachers, contemporaries, and immediate successors in the sciences (Kuhn, 1996: 3).

The history of science has been particularly prone to *teleological* explanations such as described above. This in turn has partly to do with the paradigmatic nature of the natural sciences: because competing theories are silenced within a paradigm (unlike in the social sciences), the picture that the natural sciences paint is somehow mistaken for nature itself (see Barnes, 1982: 5).

This leads us directly to the next sociologically interesting point. If teleological explanation – explaining the past through the present – was the issue in the debate between Kuhn and historians of science, the question of the relativism of scientific practice implied in *The Structure of Scientific Revolutions* was the bone of contention between Kuhn and philosophers of science. Because if the concepts of natural science are dependent on the scientific community and its conventions, the age-old idea of science as a rational quest for truth crumbles. There is no neutral – objective – point of view through which the truth or falsity of concepts can be evaluated. Although this is a sociologically interesting and valid perspective, philosophers have mostly reacted to such propositions with hostility.[8]

Interestingly enough, Kuhn's main point about 'revolutions' in science is perhaps not as sociologically fascinating as his description of 'normal science'. Revolutions happen when too many anomalies appear which cannot be accounted by the prevailing paradigm. This leads to paradigm change – that is, a scientific revolution. Sociologically speaking, this is an expected outcome of normal science and does not as such bring much new to the discussion about scientific practice. Kuhn's concept of *incommensurability* is worth noting here, however. Again, against both Whig history and the received ideas in philosophy of science, Kuhn argued that there is no way of ranking paradigms. Paradigms change because old paradigms cannot account for all the questions that arise, but that does necessarily make them less right. And in any case, we can only evaluate paradigms in their own historical, social and cultural context, not in hindsight. That is why Kuhn's work has been likened to an anthropologist's: like an anthropologist studying tribal cultures, Kuhn 'went native', trying to understand the practice of science in its own terms, 'avoiding ethnocentric evaluations and misleading analogies with his own culture' (Barnes, 1982: 5).[9]

One indicator of Kuhn's enduring influence is that his work has inspired theorizing and incited debate across disciplinary lines. Most importantly, Kuhn has argued persuasively that scientific knowledge is socially produced – socially constructed, if you will – in human interaction. Even the brilliant individual minds featured in popular histories of science make their discoveries as part of the scientific community, constrained by the conceptual frameworks of that community.[10]

Conclusion

In this chapter I have discussed the basic characteristics of social construction-ism. Although the point of the book is to draw attention to the differences between different types of constructionism, I identified three characteristics shared by the different perspectives. First, constructionisms place high value on the idea of *contingency*, that is, that the world we inhabit as individuals is not defined by our biology, psychology, or even the structure of society. Second, contingency emphasizes a sense of *liberation* that many construction-ist approaches share. This is liberation from bad ways of thinking about things or bad ways of doing things, and consequently, changing the world for the bet-ter. Finally, contingence and liberation draw attention to the *social processes* in which ideas and practices are constructed. It is no accident that so many constructionist studies employ the gerund (the verb in its *-ing* form) in the title, as in *Constructing Social Problems* (Spector and Kitsuse, 2001). I also identi-fied what could be called the four 'functions' of constructionism. First, there is the *ontological* function that tells us what the world is like, what it consists of. Second, there is the *epistemological* function that offers a view of how knowledge of the world is produced. Third, there is the *critical* function, that identifies the ways in which the world can be changed by thinking and com-municating differently about it. Finally, there is the *methodological* function that tells us how best study the processes of social construction. I argued that all the above point to the centrality of discourse in understanding social con-structionisms.

I discussed two examples that demonstrate how what we take as objective 'fact' is social in origin. In everyday life, the idea of construction is well cap-tured by W.I. Thomas's notion of 'definition of the situation': if people define situations as real, they are real in their consequences. This was certainly the case with the 'satanic panic' at a high school prom in 1980s Pennsylvania. Rumours of a satanic cult planning to kill students at the prom led to cross-county mobilization of parents, teachers, and law enforcement personnel to counter a threat that was based on (quite incredible-sounding) word of mouth. But, just as the idea that the sun revolves around the earth made sense in the sixteenth century, the satanic cult threat made sense in the framework of conservative Christianity and the symbolism used by some 'metalhead' teens that seemed to confirm the reality of Satan-worship. Like the scientists debating a theory, the facts of the Satanism case were socially 'constructed'. In the case of science, I discussed the case of Thomas Kuhn's path-breaking (indeed, paradigm-changing) book *The Structure of Scientific Revolutions* (1962) and its impact on our understanding of scientific discovery. Kuhn showed how scientific theories, even when wrong in hindsight, made complete sense at the time of their origin. Scientific knowledge is, then, not simply about getting closer to the 'truth', but a process where the 'facts' are negotiated and rethought within the scientific community.

It is now time to turn to the specific traditions of constructionism and their differences.

The Construction of Everyday Life: The Sociology of Knowledge

2

In the previous chapter I discussed the importance of what was referred to as 'taken for granted reality' or 'common sense'. This is the everyday reality of our lives that we experience and share with other people. As academic students and scholars we are one step removed from that everyday reality and can examine life from a broader perspective, as I did in the case studies of scientific revolutions and Satanism scares. But after we leave the class and step into the 'normal' world, we again assume a different approach – an everyday approach – to what is going on around us. Despite the fact that as students and scholars we might have become wary of taken-for-granted knowledge and truths, in everyday interaction (at the supermarket, at dinner with the family, and so on) we are most likely to continue to act as we always have. This is because our everyday life is the 'paramount reality' (Schutz, 1980) we live in.

The Social Construction of Reality by Peter L. Berger and Thomas Luckmann was one of the first systematic examinations of the nature of everyday knowledge from a sociological perspective, and established 'social construction' as a permanent part of the vocabulary of social science. Even if 'constructionism' has since become to denote a diverse set of traditions – the theme of *this* book – Berger and Luckmann's book can be considered the original explicitly 'constructionist' study.

First published in 1966, *The Social Construction of Reality* did not at first have much impact on the contemporary academic world. As Berger himself (1992) reminisces, the book came out at a time of widely shared dissatisfaction with the mainstream of American sociology dominated by Talcott Parsons and a narrow positivist approach. Berger and Luckmann's book was, however, overshadowed by Marxist sociology that rose to prominence both in Europe and the United States in the latter half of the 1960s. For Berger, this was one of the 'deformations' of sociology (the first being the 'methodological fetishism' of the Parsonsian school) which in his eyes undermined the credibility of the whole discipline by compromising the objectivity of social science in the name of social activism (Berger, 2002). Moreover, to the annoyance of both Berger and Luckmann (Berger, 1986; 2001; Luckmann, 2001), many of the socially active scholars employed the idea of social construction in their critique of existing power relations and stereotypical understandings of social issues. Whether or not read in ways the authors themselves would prefer, *The Social Construction of Reality* has become a widely read classic (see Hunter and Ainlay, 1986).

Berger and Luckmann did not generate their ideas in a vacuum. *The Social Construction of Reality* is full of references to classical sociological thinkers such as Karl Marx, Émile Durkheim and Max Weber. The influence of Alfred Schutz, who taught at the New School of Social Research in New York at the time when both Berger and Luckmann studied there, is especially significant (see Berger, 2001). Schutz's combination of sociology and phenomenology (Schutz, 1980; Schutz and Luckmann, 1973; 1989) influenced both authors, and it has been even suggested that *The Social Construction of Reality* represents the systematic exposition of Schutz's ideas that Schutz himself never wrote (Heiskala, 2000: 149).

By defining their project as 'a treatise in sociology of knowledge' – also the subtitle of the book – Berger and Luckmann intentionally broadened the meaning of 'knowledge' to include 'everything that passes for knowledge in society' (Berger and Luckmann, 1967: 14–15). Thus defined, Berger and Luckmann's sociology of knowledge differs significantly from the work of their predecessors, especially that of Karl Mannheim (1936), whose sociology of knowledge was based primarily on the analysis of intellectual elites and their 'ideas' (Abercrombie, 1986: 13–14). However, as the authors state in the beginning of their study, these kind of theoretical 'ideas' make up only a fragment of what passes for 'knowledge' in society. Therefore, everyday knowledge should be the focus of sociology of knowledge proper (Berger and Luckmann, 1967: 14–15). Starting from a modest-sounding sociology of knowledge perspective, Berger and Luckmann's approach in fact becomes a fully fledged theory of society and a reformulation of the core questions in sociology (Abercrombie, 1986: 26; cf. Berger, 1963).

At the centre of Berger and Luckmann's work is the classic question of sociology: is society a human product or are humans the product of society? In contemporary 'common sense' understanding we tend to consider people as individuals who by acting collectively form a society. This was also the starting point of Max Weber's sociology. Subjective meanings and ideas are the basis of human action for Weber (1978: 4). Meaningful human action in turn is the basis of institutions, and therefore the foundation of social structure. Waving one's hand does not mean anything in itself unless it is done in order to greet others. Of course the hand is waved in greeting only if other actors recognize the waving as a greeting and respond to it accordingly. When this happens, the 'institution of greeting' is established. However, from a Weberian perspective, it could not exist without the subjective meanings attached to it.

Émile Durkheim, another early pioneer of sociology, approached the question of action and structure from an opposite perspective from Weber. For Durkheim, individual identities were derived from the collective: society transcends the individual; being part of society is what makes us human (Durkheim, 1995: 436–37; Luckmann, 1967: 12–19). What Durkheim termed 'collective representations' precede individual concepts and condition the actions of individuals. Therefore, from a Durkheimian perspective, to study the meaning of hand-waving as greeting, one must focus on the traditions of the society and how those traditions are passed down to new generations. From this perspective, subjective meanings are subordinate to the social and cultural structure which ultimately determines the use of hand waving as a greeting gesture. Hand waving as an 'institution of greeting' is a *social fact*, existing outside and independent of individuals (Durkheim, 1982: 38–46).

The above description of Weber and Durkheim's ideas is necessarily simplified,[1] but it is widely acknowledged that neither of the classic formulations of the nature of the social has been completely satisfactory by itself (for example, Giddens, 1979). Inspired by the enduring problem, the question that Berger and Luckmann pose is: How can society be understood as an independent structural entity without forgetting the importance of the individual actor? In their approach, the task of unravelling this question falls to the sociology of knowledge, which concerns itself with 'world-building', that is, the process whereby 'subjective meanings *become* objective facticities' (Berger and Luckmann, 1967: 19; emphasis in the original). In other words: *'the sociology of knowledge is concerned with the analysis of the social construction of reality'* (Berger and Luckmann, 1967: 3; emphasis in the original).

World-building

Berger and Luckmann offer their own solution to the problem of social structure and individual agency by positing that *both* constitute society. Their perspective is summarized in the following sentences: *'Society is a human product. Society is an objective reality. Man is a social product'* (Berger and Luckmann, 1967: 61; emphasis in the original). This process of world-building comprises three dialectical 'moments' in which reality is socially constructed: externalization, objectivation and internalization. I will now outline each of these stages.

Externalization

Externalization can be characterized as a human being's 'continuous outpouring of himself into the world in which he finds himself' (Berger, 1973: 14). This means that humans assign meaning to the world around them and to their actions in relation to that world. When these meanings become shared, the world outside the individual actors attains an independent status. It is perceived as existing outside any individual or community. In this sense, society is a human product. How is social order achieved, then? In Berger and Luckmann's words: 'social order is a human product, or, more precisely, an ongoing human production. It is produced by man in the course of his ongoing externalization' (Berger and Luckmann, 1967: 52). The key term here is institutionalization, which proceeds in several stages.

Even the most basic survival skills are subject to meaning-making and externalization. When the proverbial solitary human on the proverbial desert island feels hungry, she learns – purportedly by trial and error since we can't assume her having any prior learned knowledge of survival – that fish satisfy her hunger. From now on whenever she feels hungry, she goes fishing without having every time to contemplate anew on what to do when she feels hungry. This is what Berger and Luckmann call habitualization. Habitualization occurs when any type of action is 'repeated frequently [and] becomes cast into a pattern' (Berger and Luckmann, 1967: 53). Furthermore, to be habitualized, a pattern must be perceived as a pattern by the actor.

Habitualization precedes institutionalization proper. Even the actions of solitary humans become habitualized. However, situations such as that of the above-mentioned lone dweller on the desert island are empirically unavailable or highly unlikely in the contemporary world. We live in constant interaction with other humans, which entails the continual ordering of not only our own actions but also the actions of others. In interaction we learn to predict the actions of others and share their meaning.

Typification is the process where we create sense and predictability for the actions of others. For example, having learned through repetition that winking an eye in certain social settings can be interpreted as a signal of interest, the subject of these signals forms an idea what is happening ('he is hitting on me') and also most likely a mental image of the winker ('he is an unsophisticated fool'). When the winker's intentions match the expectations of the subject ('I am hitting on her'), he also makes an assessment of her character and disposition ('she wants me') – the correctness of the assessment notwithstanding. Whatever the actual outcome of the situation, the fact that both parties habitually recognize and reciprocally typify the situation as 'courting' constitutes the institution of courting. In Berger and Luckmann's words: 'Institutionalization occurs whenever there is a reciprocal typification of habitualized actions by types of actors. Put differently, any such typification is an institution' (Berger and Luckmann, 1967: 54).

As the above quote implies, institutionalization entails not only the typification of actions, but also of actors. In addition to existing as typical actions, institutions are embodied in *roles* (Berger and Luckmann, 1967: 72–9). Let us think, for example, that the man in the above courting example is a university student and the woman his teacher, a professor at the university. In the classroom he is acting the role of student, taking notes and replying when deemed proper by the situation. Outside that context, while winking an eye to the professor at a nightclub, his main role is that of a 'man looking for company'. Needless to say, as the example itself demonstrates, roles are often overlapping: it would be difficult, if not impossible, for anyone to disregard the fact that the person he or she is winking at is his or her teacher at the university.

Objectivation

The process of externalization highlights the importance of face-to-face inter-action in Berger and Luckmann's theory. A face-to-face situation is a 'proto-typical case of social interaction' and '[a]ll other cases are derivatives of it' (Berger and Luckmann, 1967: 28). People are 'fully real' to each other only in these shared moments of 'here and now'. For Berger and Luckmann the face-to-face situation is the starting point for understanding how institutions come to achieve an independent status and become 'social facts' in the Durkheimian sense.

As long as the face-to-face interaction happens between members of a closed collective, institutions are more or less provisional. They achieve a new level of objectivity when the collective encounters people not familiar with its institutions. The most basic example of this is the birth of children. When knowledge of the institutions is passed on to a new generation the institutions become detached from the actors and their actions and achieve an independ-ent status. The institutions attain a historical reality outside and beyond the control of individuals. To the members of the next generation, institutions appear as taken-for-granted reality: they have been there long before the indi-viduals' own existence and will continue existing after their death. At the same time, this has a 'mirror effect' on the parents, who also begin to regard the institutions constructed in face-to-face interaction as objective reality. In this stage institutionalization progresses from the realization of 'there we go again' to 'this is how these things are done'. This is what Berger and Luckmann call the objectivation of the social world (Berger and Luckmann, 1967: 57–61).

For example, when the institution of (monogamous) marriage becomes his-torically established, individuals cannot wish it away no matter how much they would like to share their affections with people outside the marriage. If they still wish to do so, they are subject to the sanctions that the institution of marriage posits for infidelity. The institution of marriage loses its transparent nature, that is, it is not regarded as a matter of convention anymore, but as something confronting individuals (couples in this case) from 'the outside'. To the members of the next generation, the institution of marriage appears even more as *the* way of doing things, since they did not take part in its construc-tion in the first place (Berger and Luckmann, 1967: 59).

In Berger and Luckmann's vocabulary, objectivation means the 'thickening' and 'sedimentation' of the social world. In fact, 'only at this point does it become possible to speak of a social world at all' in the Durkheimian sense of a 'social fact' that confronts individuals as an objective external reality (Berger and Luckmann, 1967: 59). The attitude of 'this is how things are done' gives rise to tradition, which is passed down to future generations. Language is nat-urally the most important vehicle and 'depository' of these collective sedimen-tations (Berger and Luckmann, 1967: 69).

The 'extreme form' of objectivation is what Berger and Luckmann (follow-ing Marx) call *reification*. In reification, social reality is no longer perceived as a human product but rather as a fact of nature, a result of cosmic laws, or a manifestation of divine will (Berger and Luckmann, 1967: 89). The first part of Berger and Luckmann's summarizing definition, 'society is a human product', is thereby forgotten, and the objective world is seen as something unchangeable by human action. In reification, objectivation achieves its ultimate stage: the role of meaning-making is not recognized anymore, and the social world becomes an ontological reality completely independent of human activity (Berger and Luckmann, 1967: 90).

Both institutions and roles can become reified: For those who hold a traditional view of marriage, for example, it is 'natural' that it consists of a man and a woman. This is a reified view of the (socially constructed) institution of marriage. Yet, it is being challenged – de-reified – by gay marriage and other alternative family forms. Although the de-reification process has been slow in the case of marriage, and is controversial everywhere that it has been sanctioned by the state, at least some people have begun to regard marriage as human construction and doubt the putative 'naturalness' of heterosexual marriage. It is a similar process to the de-reification of gender roles that started (in different stages and forms) with the feminist movement. The reified role of husband and wife, which assumed that women should stay home and take care of children while the husband 'earns a living', was challenged, and gender equality is now something which many societies at least strive towards, even if they're not quite there yet.

Reification is one of the most important concepts of social constructionist theory. As was noted in the introduction, we take most things in our everyday life for granted. In other words, our everyday life is largely reified. That is also why understanding social constructionism requires a certain suppression of everyday 'common sense.' It is, of course, practical not to question the objectivity of every social phenomenon all the time. In addition, it has been suggested that humans are biologically liable to reify (Berger and Luckmann, 1967: 90). Berger and Luckmann go on from these observations to point out the relative novelty and unusualness of what could be called the 'constructionist mindset': 'This implies that an apprehension of reification *as* a modality of consciousness is dependent upon an at least relative *de*reification of consciousness, which is a comparatively late development in history and in any individual biography' (Berger and Luckmann, 1967: 90; emphasis in the original).

Berger and Luckmann's claim that de-reification is a historically novel phenomenon is difficult to confirm empirically. The important point of their claim is that it emphasizes the taken-for-granted conception of social reality that children have. De-reification and the acquisition of a 'constructionist mindset' is therefore developed – if developed at all – in the course of learning and socialization, a theme that takes up much of Berger and Luckmann's discussion of the third 'moment' of the constructionist dialectic, internalization.

Internalization

It is not only among sociologists that *The Social Construction of Reality* has become a classic. Berger and Luckmann's discussion of internalization also places them in the core of social psychological theorizing. In their tripartite scheme internalization forms the third 'moment' in which individuals adopt the objective world as their own. This occurs in the process of socialization which the authors further divide into primary and secondary socialization.

Berger and Luckmann often remind the reader that the constructionist dialectic is not a temporal process which occurs in distinct stages (Berger and Luckmann, 1967: 129). Primary socialization, however, occurs in a certain phase of the individual's life, namely that of childhood. It is the basis for understanding social life and frames an individual's conception of the objective world more than any subsequent socialization (Berger and Luckmann, 1967: 134–5). Primary socialization is the 'comprehensive and consistent induction of an individual into the objective world of a society or a sector of it' (Berger and Luckmann, 1967: 130).

Compared to later, secondary socializations, the most significant aspect of primary socialization is that children cannot choose the world which they internalize (Berger and Luckmann, 1967: 134–5). Instead, 'the world,' the paramount objective reality is posited to them by the 'significant others' who (at least in the modern Western context) are often the biological parents of the child, but may also be other people who are central to the internalization process.[2] Children learn the definitions, attitudes and roles of their parents and subsequently internalize the world they mutually inhabit (Berger and Luckmann, 1967: 132). The view of the world transmitted by parents' definitions is, furthermore, affected by social structure. Differences in education and income, for instance, shape the image passed down to the next generation (Berger and Luckmann, 1967: 131). For example, the children of working-class parents are likely to have different hobbies and attitudes towards work and education than their middle-class counterparts.[3]

Berger and Luckmann emphasize that internalization is a lifelong continuous process. It is never possible – even in relatively simple societies – to internalize all of the objectivated social reality (Berger and Luckmann, 1967: 134). Primary socialization, however, does have an end, at least as a phase in childhood. For Berger and Luckmann the end of primary socialization is the moment when the individual becomes aware of the wider framework of social life. This happens when the individual 'identifies not only with concrete others but with a generality of others, that is, with society' (Berger and Luckmann, 1967: 133). This 'generalized other' is a 'progressive abstraction from the roles and attitudes of specific others to roles and attitudes *in general*' (Berger and Luckmann, 1967: 132; emphasis in the original). They elaborate the point with a concrete example of a very basic feature of socialization, table manners:

[I]n the internalization of norms there is a progression from 'Mummy is angry with me *now*' to 'Mummy is angry with me *whenever* I spill the soup.' As additional significant others (father, grandmother, older sister, and so on) support the mother's negative attitude toward soup-spilling, the generality of the norm is subjectively extended. The decisive step comes when the child recognizes that *everybody* is against soup-spilling, and the norm is generalized to '*One* does not spill soup' – 'one' being himself as part of a generality that includes, in principle, *all* of society insofar as it is significant to the child (Berger and Luckmann, 1967: 132–3; emphases in the original).

The awareness of the generalized other also marks the formation of identity, which is one of the most important concepts of social psychology (see Chapter 4). In Berger and Luckmann's terms, identity is formed when an individual's self-identification becomes stable and continuous, and reflects an understanding of his or her role and place in the overall society, not just in relation to the significant others (Berger and Luckmann, 1967: 137).

Berger and Luckmann define secondary socialization as the 'internalization of institutional or institution-based "subworlds"' (Berger and Luckmann, 1967: 138). This includes learning the norms and roles of the school, the workplace, or whatever institution individuals interact with later in their lives. Secondary socializations are always superimposed on the primarily socialized world and are thus subjectively less inevitable. Unlike the self that is constructed in primary socialization, the self of secondary socialization is partial and role-specific. For example, I can be a very effective tax-collector, but after the working day is over I may be extremely critical of tax laws and the problems that certain kind of taxation causes for certain kind of people.

In addition to the fact that we are able to – at least to a certain extent – choose and influence our secondary socializations, another significant difference between primary and secondary socialization is that primary socialization is not only cognitive, but also emotional. That is why Berger and Luckmann conclude that marginal life situations (death, for example) tend to be profound challenges to the internalizations of primary socialization, whereas the reality of secondary socialization tends to be trivialized in such situations. In their words:

[I]t may be said that the imminence of death profoundly threatens the reality of one's previous self-identification as a man, a moral being, or a Christian. One's self-identification as an assistant manager in the ladies' hosiery department is not so much threatened as trivialized in the same situation (Berger and Luckmann, 1967: 148).

Because of its more detached and therefore less 'ultimately real' nature, secondary socialization and the roles assigned to individuals by it can be challenged more easily. Berger and Luckmann illustrate this by stating that:

A relatively minor shift in the subjective definition of reality would suffice for an individual to take for granted that one may go to the office without a tie. A much more drastic shift would be necessary to have him go, as a matter of course, without any clothes at all (Berger and Luckmann, 1967: 148).

Some psychologically oriented perspectives might point out the 'innate' sense of shame that humans feel without clothes. Berger and Luckmann do not deny that this sense of shame exists (1967: 148), but that shame is also shaped by social definitions. Primary and secondary socialization are both social constructions, even though the internalization of the rules on nudity, for example, may seem to be more in the 'nature of things.' However, if we look at the status of women in history, for example, we can readily see that some very deeply held – that is to say, primarily socialized – assumptions about the 'nature of things' can be and have been changed.

World-maintenance

The three moments of Berger and Luckmann's scheme described above outline the process whereby reality is constructed in social interaction. However, as I have already mentioned in passing, no socially constructed world is a stable creation, they are all ever changing. After social worlds have been constructed they need to be continuously maintained by those inhabiting them; otherwise they risk a 'lapse' back into a chaotic state of unorderliness. In other words, the particular institutions created in the construction process need to be legitimated.

The importance of legitimation has been already alluded to in the beginning of the discussion on objectivation. As long as an institution is based on simple habitualization and shared typifications, it does not need to be legitimated. But when somebody outside the immediate sphere of experience – a second-generation child, for example – enters the picture, the budding institution becomes historical and needs to be explained and justified to the second generation which does not share the experience of the original habitualization (Berger and Luckmann, 1967: 93). Legitimation explains *why* an institution is as it is, and also why it *should* be as it is. Therefore it has a both a cognitive (explanatory) and a normative (justificatory) function (Berger and Luckmann, 1967: 93–4).

Levels of legitimation

Berger and Luckmann differentiate between four levels of legitimation. These levels overlap continuously in everyday life, but the distinction makes explicit how legitimation actually works. The levels Berger and Luckmann discuss are: (1) incipient legitimation, (2) rudimentary theoretical propositions, (3) explicit theory, and (4) symbolic universes.

So far I have not discussed the role of language in Berger and Luckmann's theory. The authors make clear the importance of language from the outset of their study (1967: 22, 34–41), but compared to the later developments of constructionist thought, especially those perspectives focusing on the analysis of discourse (see Chapters 4 and 5), *The Social Construction of Reality* does not dwell extensively on language and how language should be analysed in order to study the processes of social construction. However, in the context of incipient legitimation, language is the focus of attention. In Berger and Luckmann's terms incipient legitimation is present everywhere in our everyday speech. Legitimating explanations 'are, so to speak, built into the vocabulary' (Berger and Luckmann, 1967: 94). For example, the word 'cousin' is taken for granted to imply a simple relation to a family member. But it also carries with it a sense that refers to restrictions of sexual relations between certain family members, imputed rights of inheritance, and so forth. Outside one's immediate sphere of experience, language is the most important legitimating mechanism. Without language, functioning in a complex social system would be impossible. Although it might be tempting to see language as a neutral vehicle for communication, it is always legitimating in nature simply because it inherently functions as an objectivation of the world (Berger and Luckmann, 1967: 22, 94–5).

Discussing the second level of legitimation, Berger and Luckmann describe elements of everyday speech such as proverbs, moral maxims and wise sayings. These the authors term collectively as 'theoretical propositions in a rudimentary form' (Berger and Luckmann, 1967: 94). The difference with explicit theories is that these rudimentary theoretical propositions are always related to a very practical purpose. Wise sayings and folk tales often include a moral lesson, which is invoked for the purpose of legitimating a certain course of action – or instructing others to refrain from a certain course of action. The famous tale of the Three Little Pigs, where the Big Bad Wolf huffs and puffs down the two hastily built houses of the first two pigs but not the sturdy house of the oldest one, can be interpreted as a moral tale about the value of hard work. As Bruno Bettelheim puts it in his famous book, *The Uses of Enchantment* (1977: 41–2):

> [The tale] teaches ... that we must not be lazy and take things easy, for if we do, we may perish. Intelligent planning and foresight combined with hard labor will make us victorious over even our most ferocious enemy – the wolf! The story also shows the advantages of growing up, since the third and wisest pig is usually depicted as the biggest and oldest.

The third level is comprised of explicit theories. These are legitimations of different sectors of society which have developed into a specialized and differentiated body of knowledge (Berger and Luckmann, 1967: 94). Often the formulation and maintenance of explicit theories is designated to a certain group of experts, whether they are tribe elders or social service professionals. Each of

these is responsible for devising a system of explanation and justification pertaining to a specific sector of society, for example, cousinhood (tribe elders) or
eligibility for social security (social service professionals).

Symbolic universes are the most comprehensive of all forms of legitimation,
and comprise the fourth level in Berger and Luckmann's schema. While all of
the previously described levels of legitimation more or less deal with concrete,
everyday situations, symbolic universes form the framework that answers
questions of 'ultimate meaning', such as 'Who am I?', 'Where do we come
from?' and so forth. In addition, symbolic universes make the whole of social
reality meaningful to the individual by ordering it into a 'system'. Put more
formally, a symbolic universe is 'a body of tradition that integrates a large
number of definitions of reality and presents the institutional order to the individual as a symbolic totality' (Berger, Berger and Kellner, 1973: 109). Religion,
for example, gives the social order legitimacy on a cosmic scale: the institutional order is not only a human invention, but the will of gods. Similarly, individual questions of 'ultimate' meaning, for example 'What happens to me after
I die?', are answered by religion. The concept of symbolic universes thus
comes very close to the perhaps more familiar term worldview (Luckmann,
1967: 51–53; Berger et al., 1973: 109).

Symbolic universes are explanations and justifications which encompass *all*
features of society; by integrating everything within their explanatory framework, they legitimate the institutional order on the highest possible level of
generality (Berger and Luckmann, 1967: 104). Symbolic language transcends
everyday reality, making it possible to legitimate the institutional order by
referring to theoretical ideas and worldviews that are not empirically available
(Berger and Luckmann, 1967: 40, 95–6). Religion, philosophy, and science are
the most important examples of symbolic universes (Berger and Luckmann,
1967: 110–12; Abercrombie, 1986: 21). I will return to the case of religion in
more detail later in the chapter.

It is unclear which level of legitimation Berger and Luckmann consider
most important. In *The Social Construction of Reality* they dwell longest on
the level of symbolic universes, but in his later work Berger (1973: 39) emphasizes the significance of the pre-theoretical level and language. The latter seems
intuitively to be more important because in everyday life we cannot escape language. Language is, however, a site for competing legitimations, whereas symbolic universes tend to shut out competition by virtue of their totality. For
example, religion has been historically the most effective tool for legitimating
and therefore reifying the existing social order (Abercrombie, 1986: 21; see
below).

Individual world-maintenance

Because socialization is never complete, even in relatively simple societies,
legitimation aims to ensure that the objective definitions of reality are effectively shared among individuals. However, in addition to this, individuals need

to order and maintain their subjective reality. In Berger and Luckmann's vocabulary, legitimation works 'horizontally' by integrating individuals into the totality of social institutions – that is, assigning them roles and situating them in the complex network of roles – and 'vertically' by making the institutional order subjectively meaningful in the individual's biography (Berger and Luckmann, 1967: 92–3). The legitimation on the subjective or 'vertical' level is what Berger (1973) calls world-maintenance.[4]

Socialization makes everyday life subjectively meaningful, and is successful when the objective world is more or less taken for granted in individual consciousness. Everyday interaction is the most efficient way of subjective world-maintenance. The nightmares of the previous night are relegated to the realm of dreams when the 'paramount' reality of everyday life is confronted in the bus on the way to work, while greeting a colleague in the workplace, and so on (Berger and Luckmann, 1967: 147–50). Furthermore, in conversation, individuals reaffirm their subjective reality by repeating familiar routine comments on the current weather, yesterday's news and anticipation about the upcoming football match. These everyday routines create a feeling of continuity, which is one of the most important features of subjective world-maintenance.

The importance of the continuity of everyday routine is well exemplified in Harold Garfinkel's (1963; 1967) experiments with everyday conversation. Garfinkel asked his students to monitor their friends' and relatives' reactions when taken-for-granted ways of conversation were suddenly called into question by the student conducting the experiment. Many of the examples concern situations of everyday talk that, instead of confirming routine patterns of behaviour, disrupt the everyday routine – resulting often in angry response from the subjects of the experiments. Here are two illustrative examples (from Heritage, 1984: 80):

Case 1: The subject (S) was telling the experimenter (E), a member of the subject's carpool, about having had a flat tire while going to work the previous day.
S: I had a flat tire.
E: What do you mean you had a flat tire?
S: [She appeared momentarily stunned. Then she answered in a hostile way.] What do you mean? What do you mean? A flat tire is a flat tire. That is what I meant. Nothing special. What a crazy question!

Case 6: The victim waved his hand cheerily.
S: How are you?
E: How am I in regard to what? My health, my finance, my school work, my peace of mind, my...
S: [Red in the face and suddenly out of control.] Look! I was just trying to be polite. Frankly, I don't give a damn how you are.

As the above interruptions of routine behaviour demonstrate, the world-main-tenance that occurs in everyday interaction is mostly implicit. There are, how-ever, moments in life when explicit measures are required to maintain the integrity of the subjective world. These explicit maintenance measures may be either individual or collective. For individuals, this kind of 'crisis maintenance' occurs especially in 'marginal' life situations, of which the encounter with death is the most important (Berger and Luckmann, 1967: 156; Berger, 1973: 60). In addition, 'society itself sets up specific procedures for situations recog-nized as involving the risk of breakdown in reality' (Berger and Luckmann, 1967: 156). These situations can include coping with natural disasters, threat of violence, or confronting 'the other' – that is, someone of different creed, colour, sexual orientation and so on. Crisis maintenance often takes the form of explicit rituals, ranging from religious feasts to mediated events of social significance (Berger and Luckmann, 1967: 156; see Bellah, 1967; Dayan and Katz, 1988).

Viable world-maintenance is dependent on a shared understanding of real-ity that is being reproduced in interaction, whether everyday conversation (routine maintenance) or elaborate ritual (crisis maintenance). These shared understandings are what Berger (1970: 34–7; Berger and Luckmann, 1967: 157) calls plausibility structures:

> [P]lausibility, in the sense of what people actually find credible, of views of reality depends on the social support these receive. Put more simply, we obtain our notions about the world originally from other human beings, and these notions continue to be plausible to us in a very large measure because others continue to affirm them (Berger, 1970: 43).

Plausibility structures are formed in various social networks which have vary-ing definitions of reality. Therefore, the plausibility structure pertaining to, for example, homosexual identity differs greatly between a gay community and a conservative Christian community. But on a more general level – such as that of everyday manners in face-to-face interaction – a plausibility structure may encompass all or most members of a society.

For most of the time individuals are affected by the same plausibility struc-tures for their whole lives, but subjective world-maintenance is challenged by changes both in the individual's biography and surrounding social conditions. Moving permanently to a different culture is increasingly common nowadays, and often calls for resocialization at some level. Rapid social change, such as that taking place in the former socialist states of Eastern Europe, also has a powerful effect on plausibility structures and therefore the world-maintenance of individuals.

While the subjective reality is transformed in all of the above cases, we rarely speak of total identity change. My friend Jane is still the same Jane even if she lives in Saudi-Arabia and wears a veil. There are, however, instances where the transformation is so powerful that it can be said that the individual 'switches worlds' (Berger and Luckmann, 1967: 157). This means resocialization on the primary level. Extreme transformations such as this differ from original primary socialization in that they are always built on a pre-existing subjective reality and therefore require the 'undoing' of at least part of previous primary socializations. However, extreme transformations resemble primary socialization more than secondary socialization, mainly because of the affective dimension often lacking in secondary socialization. Alcoholics Anonymous is a good example of a powerful transformation process at the primary level. Resocialization into a substance-free life is supported by a shared plausibility structure and a system of 'mutual self-help' to prevent lapses (Mäkelä et al., 1996; Arminen, 1998; see Berger, 1970: 35). Another prototypical example of extreme transformation is religious conversion.

The legitimating agencies of society

As described above, legitimation is an ever-present process, which occurs first and foremost on the level of everyday language. In addition, there are certain institutions of society that are specifically equipped to legitimate the existing social order, the family being the first and most important socializing institution. However, the primary socialization occurring in family settings is often implicit, in the sense that parents, for example, are rarely explicitly aware of the totality of knowledge and values passed down to the next generation. This kind of informal education does not have a curriculum.

Formal comprehensive and state-funded education has become an almost universal feature of modern societies. Concurrently, the school system has become a very important site for the legitimation of the social order. Because the function of education in society is to pass down tradition, it is by definition 'conservative' in the sense that it legitimates existing definitions of social reality. However, the autonomy of education (from political, religious, or other influences) implies that no particular definition of reality is prevalent in the school system. Therefore, at least in principle, the state-funded school system is not conservative or liberal, religious or irreligious. If any of these options is preferred, a system of private education, such as Catholic schooling, exists alongside state-funded schools.

The nominal autonomy of state-funded education does not, however, mean that the school system is neutral and produces equally qualified members of society. A number of influential studies of state-funded education (especially Bourdieu and Passeron, 1990) have forcefully argued that the success of the secondary socialization into the school system is heavily dependent on primary socialization. This means that a student's social background is a major indicator of his or her success in the school system. Individuals coming from families where formal education is not valued are more likely to fare badly in school and not continue to the higher levels which could open opportunities for better jobs (Willis, 1978). This way the state-funded school system actually reinforces and legitimates the existing constructions of social order, making it one of the most potent legitimating agencies of society.

Case study: The social reality of religion

In addition to *The Social Construction of Reality*, both Peter Berger and Thomas Luckmann have written extensively on religion in the contemporary world. It is therefore fitting to discuss the application of their sociology of knowledge to the phenomenon of religion. In doing so, I am relying primarily on Peter Berger's best-known work *The Sacred Canopy*.[5]

Religion as a sacred canopy

Speaking of Berger and Luckmann's concept of symbolic universes, Nicholas Abercrombie (1986: 21) states: 'Religion is, historically, the most obviously successful symbolic universe' (see Berger, 1973: 36–7). Although the truth claims of religion may have become increasingly problematic as a consequence of challenging explanations brought about by modernization, Berger keenly illustrates why religion has been and still continues to be a powerful way of legitimating everyday life.

At the heart of Berger's theorizing on religion are the same assumptions about human nature already described in *The Social Construction of Reality*. However, in *The Sacred Canopy* the human experience of chaos and the need for order is emphasized perhaps even more than in his previous works. In addition, the terms Berger uses are somewhat different in appearance, if not in content, from the ones used in *The Social Construction of Reality*. The four concepts central to the understanding of religion as a social phenomenon à la Berger are (1) anomy, (2) theodicy, (3) alienation and (4) plausibility structure.

The influence of Émile Durkheim is evident in Berger's use of the term anomy (Berger, 1973: 31–4; cf. Durkheim, 1979: 258). For Berger, anomy means terror in the face of disorder, senselessness and madness which threatens to make human existence meaningless (Berger, 1973: 32). The human need for meaning-making, introduced in *The Social Construction of Reality*, is an attempt to shield against the horror of anomy. People have multiple ways of explaining anomy and ordering and legitimating their social reality. When the 'human condition' is explained as a result of God's creation, for example, the explanation is a theodicy: 'an explanation of [anomic] phenomena in terms of religious legitimations, of whatever degree of theoretical sophistication, may be called a theodicy' (Berger, 1973: 61; Campbell, 2001: 77).[6] In other words, theodicy is world-maintenance in a religious framework.

But what constitutes a 'religious framework' in Berger's theory? Although he never sets out to formulate a strict definition of religion, the clues given in *The Sacred Canopy* show that Berger's conception of religion is thoroughly permeated by his understanding of the world as a product of human interaction and the basic human need for order:

> [Religion is] the establishment, through human activity, of an all-embracing sacred order, that is, of a sacred cosmos that will be capable of maintaining itself in the ever-present face of chaos ... Every human society is, in the last resort, men banded together in the face of death. The power of religion depends, in the last resort, upon the credibility of the banners it puts in the hands of men as they stand before death, or more accurately, as they walk inevitably towards it (Berger, 1973: 59–60).

Religion is a symbolic universe that legitimates the social order on a cosmic scale: human existence becomes part of a larger scheme of things in which the spiritual side of life is an integral part. This 'spirituality' can manifest itself in a myriad of forms, from Christian belief in the redeeming power of Christ to the devising of astrological charts to foretell one's future (see Heelas and Woodhead, 2005; Wuthnow, 1998; Roof, 1999). Similar ordering is evident also in the secular sphere: for some, 'personal philosophies of life, scientific world-views, secular philosophies such as Marxism and nihilism, or common-sensical ideas about luck and fate' (Wuthnow, 1986: 127) fulfil the same function as religion.

For Berger, however, religion is different from all other symbolic universes because of its special alienating nature. Alienation, a concept derived from Karl Marx (1961: 175–185; Ollman, 1976; see Berger, 1973: 204n5), refers to a process 'whereby the dialectical relationship between the individual and his world is lost to consciousness' (Berger, 1973: 92). Berger elaborates further:

> The individual 'forgets' that this world was and continues to be co-produced by him. Alienated consciousness is undialectical consciousness. The essential difference between the socio-cultural world and the world of nature is obscured – namely, the difference that men have made the first but not the second (Berger, 1973: 92).

Defined in this way, alienation comes very close to Berger and Luckmann's concept of reification (see above, Berger and Luckmann, 1967: 89–90). Whether reification refers to a specific instance of a general alienated state of consciousness, as some have suggested (Abercrombie, 1986: 17), or whether the terms are interchangeable is not of importance here. What is essential is that alienation represents an extreme form of objectivation whereby the constructed nature of the social world is obscured. Religion has a very powerful alienating effect because it places the ultimate reality outside of human experience, into the divine sphere. The 'overwhelming otherness' of religious legitimation mystifies the process of human world-building and, consequently, 'the humanly made world is explained in terms that deny its human production' (Berger, 1973: 95–6).

Religions make claims that are not empirically testable. Modern science has repudiated many of the claims endorsed by traditional religious worldviews, yet most people on earth profess some religion. Why do religious explanations persevere in spite of opposite evidence? Furthermore, there are hundreds of different religions competing in the worldview market. How can people know that their religion is the 'true' religion? Berger's concept of plausibility structures (see above) focuses attention on the social networks that maintain the plausibility of religious beliefs even when they are challenged by competing explanations. Therefore – as a human endeavour – religions are plausible only if maintained by plausibility structures and rituals that strengthen these structures (Berger, 1970: 34–8).

Religion and the 'disenchantment of the world' in history

So far, Berger's remarks on religion have moved on a highly abstract level, congruently with his theorizing about the nature of social knowledge. However, his premier contribution to the sociology of religion has been his discussion of the role of religion in history and in particular the process of secularization. Berger defines secularization as 'the process by which sectors of society and culture are removed from the domination of religious institutions and symbols' (Berger, 1973: 113). He goes on:

> [I]n modern Western history, of course, secularization manifests itself in the evacuation by the Christian Churches of areas previously under their control or influence – as in the separation of church and state, or in the expropriation of church lands, or in the emancipation of education from ecclesiastical authority (Berger, 1973: 113).

This type of secularization can be called alternatively structural or objective secularization, as it pertains specifically to the differentiation of social institutions and the 'location' of religion in the objectivated structure of society (cf. Hammond, 1986: 146; Hervieu-Léger, 2001). But as Berger's own definition of secularization already implies, 'secularization is more than a social-structural process' (Berger, 1973: 113). In addition to structural changes, secularization has a significant effect on culture, or the sphere of 'ideas' – most important which is the rise of science as an independent and inherently secular perspective on the world.

Another type of secularization, closely related to the structural processes described above, is what Berger refers to as subjective secularization, or the secularization of consciousness. In this type of secularization, religion ceases to be plausible at the individual level. The 'ultimate' meaning is not provided by religion anymore, but by secular alternatives – if provided at all (Berger, 1973: 113).

Differentiating between the two types of secularization, it can be concluded that structural secularization does not necessarily entail loss of religion as such, but its relocation from the public to the private sphere (Luckmann, 1967; Berger, 1973: 114). Secularization of consciousness, however, implies that religious answers to questions of meaning become increasingly less plausible, and possibly entirely irrelevant, for individuals. The relation between the two types of secularization is, of course, complex, and the two are always intermingled. A look at the possible sources of secularization that Berger discusses in *The Sacred Canopy* sheds some light on the dialectics between structural secularization and the secularization of consciousness.

For Berger the two most important 'carriers' of secularization in the Western world are the capitalist economy and the Western religious tradition – Protestant Christianity in particular – itself (see Weber, 2001). The development of the capitalist economy in the West has brought about two important changes in relation to religion, namely social differentiation and rationalization. With differentiation, religion becomes one distinct sector of society and, consequently, as already noted: 'sectors of society and culture are removed from the domination of religious institutions and symbols' (Berger, 1973: 113). In other words, whereas in early modern Europe religion used to be part of everyday life, since the advent of capitalist economy it has become a 'Sunday affair'.

The upkeep and growth of the economic sphere also requires widespread rationalization to sustain effective production. In traditional societies pigs might have been hunted according to the standards outlined in a 'myth of pig-hunting' (see Bruce, 1996: 12). Modern economy, however, aiming at effective production and surplus above all, discards the traditional myth in order to herd the pigs and slaughter them mechanically for maximal profit. This rationalization occurs on the structural level in the creation of effective bureaucracies but also on the level of consciousness (Berger, 1973: 136). Whatever an individual's religious beliefs are, they should not be a factor in his or her functioning as a member of the production process.

The second major cause of secularization is the secularizing tendency of the 'Western religious tradition' itself. Although Berger, following Weber (2001), sees the Protestant Reformation as the pivotal turning point in the development of the secularization process, he goes further back, arguing, again like Weber, that the seeds of the 'disenchantment of the world' were already present in ancient Judaism. In contrast to the divinities of other cultures and religious traditions in the ancient Middle East, the God of the Jews was radically transcendent, something completely outside of everyday human experience. The mystery of the natural world was diminished because there was only one true god, and the spirits that use to inhabit trees, rivers, and the household, for example, lost their power and meaning – gradually, to be sure, but inevitably. In addition, this one God could not be invoked or appeased by magic-like techniques. Instead, a rationalized law (*torah*) became the guideline of everyday behaviour. Humanity's relationship with God took a completely different form with the 'demythologizing' of the natural world and the rationalization of the rules of 'the good life' (Berger, 1973: 121–30).

In Christianity, the Catholic church returned some of the mystery by positing saints as mediators between god and humanity and emphasizing the importance of some of the more 'magical' aspects of religion such as the healing power of relics. But the Reformation again stripped the church of all its mystery, positing an ultimately transcendent God who passes judgment on humanity regardless of their actions. This had radical consequences also on the ritual and material levels of religion because the Protestant churches emphasized the sermon and communal hymn singing instead of elaborate ceremony (Berger, 1973: 127–30; Smart, 1998: 336–43).

Subjective secularization, or the secularization of consciousness, is in many ways connected to structural secularization. Berger emphasizes that the structure and the individual are in a dialectic relationship, and that it important not to consider these two in terms of simple mechanistic causality (Berger, 1973: 132). However, Berger's important assertion is that structural secularization leads to pluralism (Berger, 1973: 138–9). That is to say that with structural secularization no one religious tradition has a monopoly over the individual ways of world-maintenance. In this situation, religion becomes a matter of individual choice and 'preference' – and loses its objective character in the process:

> The pluralistic situation multiplies the number of plausibility structures competing with each other. *Ipso facto*, it relativizes their religious contents. More specifically, the religious contents are 'de-objectivated', that is, deprived of their status as taken-for-granted, objective reality in consciousness. They become 'subjectivized' in a double sense: their 'reality' becomes a 'private' affair of individuals , that is, loses the quality of self-evident intersubjective plausibility ... And their 'reality' in so far as it is still maintained by the individual, is apprehended as being rooted within the consciousness of the individual rather than in any facticities of the external world (Berger, 1973: 155).

In addition to interreligious competition, religions also have to compete with secular symbolic universes and definitions of reality. Religion becomes a commodity, which can be replaced by a secular alternative. Already in *The Social Construction of Reality*, and subsequently in many of his writings, Berger points to the growing importance of psychology and psychotherapy as alternative vehicles for meaning-making in the modern (Western) world (Berger and Luckmann, 1967: 175–80; Berger, 1973: 154).

In summary, according to Berger the plausibility structures of religion diminish in a pluralistic situation. And without plausibility structures to support religious legitimations, the individual consciousness is open to secularization. In *The Sacred Canopy* and his other earlier writings Berger seems to think of secularization as a linear process which inevitably leads to the change of the structural location of religion and, ultimately, to the erosion of religion at the level of individual consciousness. Like so many other sociologists of religion of his time, Berger saw little future for religion in the modern world.

However, by the 1970s Berger had started expressing doubts about the validity of his own views on secularization (Berger et al., 1973: 199; Berger, 1977: 68). The definitive break with the 'early Berger', however, came with the publication of *The Desecularization of the World* (1999a), which Berger edited and wrote an introduction to. What the title of the books suggests, Berger bluntly states in the introduction: 'My point is that the assumption that we live in a secularized world is false' (Berger, 1999b: 2).

On a more theoretical level, Berger has changed his argument about the outcome of the pluralization process. Whereas he previously at least implied a process whereby individual consciousness would become secularized as the result of pluralism, he has later stated that 'pluralism affects the *how* of religious belief, but not necessarily the *what*' (Berger, 2001: 194; emphasis in the original). This means that religion continues to be a source for answering questions of 'ultimate meaning' for some. However, in the modern world, religion is increasingly a matter of individual choice, and is not necessarily taken to be an infallible explanation of all existence (*vis-à-vis* scientific claims, for example).

Conclusion

In this chapter I have discussed the sociology of knowledge approach to social constructionism, as exemplified by Berger and Luckmann's classic *The Social Construction of Reality*. The dialectic of social construction is summarized in their sentences 'Society is a human product. Society is an objective reality. Man is a social product.' Institutionalization – the 'sedimentation' of habits into shared patterns of action – creates 'society' that is perceived to be something external to the individual. The dialectical spiral continues in socialization, where individuals learn the ways of living in a society – and then start over by creating new institutions. This 'world-construction' needs to be continuously legitimated, so that the shared definitions of reality are effectively shared by all members of a society. Among the legitimating institutions of society is religion, which puts the current social order into a cosmic perspective, for example, when the role of women in society is legitimated by a reference to sacred texts. As a case study of how constructionist ideas have been applied to research in sociology, I discussed Berger's influential account of religion's declining importance as a world-legitimating force in modernity.

The Making of the Dark Side of Society: Social Problems as Social Constructions

3

Take a newspaper or watch the television news any given day and you will be flooded with images showing a myriad of social problems. The tabloid press, especially, is fixated on the 'dark side' of our modern societies. Therefore, it is safe to say that most of us have an idea what could be included in a list of contemporary social problems: drug abuse, crime, racial conflict and terrorism, for example, are all very visible topics in the news, politics, and in everyday talk.

The sociological study of social problems emerged, and has been particularly prominent, in American sociology. The need for a social-scientific approach to social issues arose from the practical realities of American society, which underwent a process of rapid industrialization and urbanization beginning in the late nineteenth century and accelerating at an unprecedented pace after World War I. Poverty, homelessness, unemployment and crime in the cities were some of the pressing concerns that early sociology tried to alleviate by applying results of scientific research to the phenomena (Berger and Berger, 1975: 38). Although European societies, of course, struggled with similar issues, it was in the United States where a distinct tradition for the study of social problems was born.

Especially important for this development were some prominent sociologists of the sociology department of the University of Chicago, commonly referred to as the 'Chicago School' of sociology (Carey, 1975; Bulmer, 1984; Becker, 1999). The earliest Chicago sociologists conducted large ethnographic research projects dealing with urban social problems and became known for their theories of social disorganization (Rubington and Weinberg, 1995: 53–57). More important for the development of the constructionist study of social problems were the scholars (especially Blumer, 1969) whose theoretical perspective is referred to as 'symbolic interactionism', and who inspired the post-World War II generation of scholars later dubbed 'the second Chicago school' (see Fine, 1995).

As in all disciplines, sociologists build upon the foundations their predecessors have created. The constructionist study of social problems is no different in this sense. The best way of examining how constructionist perspectives evolved from early American sociology is to examine the development of the answers given to the question 'What is a social problem?' As we will see, the definition of social problems has changed noticeably over the years, reflecting the theoretical developments in sociology.

What is a social problem?

What is a social problem? A quick look at university course syllabuses and textbook table of contents shows that same topics that interest the media (see above) seem to be considered central to teaching. But listing all possible problems does not yet give a serious student of social problems an adequate answer. Consider this: why is prostitution considered a high-priority social problem in some places (the Nordic countries, for example), and tolerated, or even supported, within limits, in others (the Netherlands, for example)? Does that make prostitution a social problem or not?

An influential definition by sociologists Richard Fuller and Richard Myers – although first published over 70 years ago – summarizes what is at stake when we talk about social problems:

> A social problem is a condition which is defined by a considerable number of persons as a deviation from some social norm which they cherish. Every social problem thus consists of an objective condition and subjective definition. The objective condition is a verifiable situation which can be checked as to existence and magnitude (proportion) by impartial and trained observers, e.g. the state of our national defense, trends in the birth rate, unemployment, etc. The subjective definition is the awareness of certain individuals that the condition is a threat to certain cherished values (Fuller and Myers, 1941: 320).

Thus, according to Fuller and Myers, for something to be considered a social problem, an objective condition – the existence of prostitution, for example – is not sufficient. People also need to define prostitution as problematic. Sometimes these two factors are not related in any straightforward way, leading to changing emphases in the definition of social problems. As theory-building developed, the focus of the study of social problems also shifted. Early sociologists were interested in the objective conditions, and firmly believed that they were the 'impartial and trained observers' capable of measuring whether a condition was a social problem or not. Later generations, however, became increasingly interested in the subjective definition part of Fuller and Myers' classic formulation.

A definitive break from earlier sociology of social problems happened in the 1960s, with several important publications endorsing a completely revised approach that became known as 'labeling theory.' Howard Becker, who is often quoted as one of the main representatives of the approach, wrote in his influential book, *The Outsiders*:

> *[S]ocial groups create deviance by making the rules whose infraction constitutes deviance*, and by applying those rules to particular people and labeling them as outsiders. From this point of view, deviance is *not* a quality of the act the person commits, but rather a consequence of the application by others of rules and sanctions to an 'offender' (Becker, 1991[1963]: 9; emphases in the original).

Becker's definition was clearly different from the prevailing understanding of deviance. For a while, research based on the labeling perspective supplanted the older approaches and became the hegemonic 'theory' in the sociology of deviance and social problems.

Some opponents of the labeling approach based their critiques on the older tradition of the study of deviance and went on conducting research that focused on the objective conditions, stating that the labeling approach simply was not adequately supported by empirical facts (for example, Akers, 2000: 126–8). Another strand of criticism, however, was inspired by the labeling approach but wanted to take it further. This strand of criticism eventually evolved into what is now known as the social constructionist perspective on social problems (Rubington and Weinberg, 1995: 287–92).

The first and most influential flag-bearers of the new approach were John I. Kitsuse and Malcolm Spector, who wrote two important articles (Kitsuse and Spector, 1973; Spector and Kitsuse, 1973) that redefined the study of social problems in the early 1970s. They later compiled their ideas into a book titled *Constructing Social Problems* (Spector and Kitsuse, 2001 [1977]), which soon became the definitive work on the constructionist perspective.

Spector and Kitsuse's argument was that although the labeling perspective had rightly emphasized subjective definitions over objective conditions, Becker and others did not take the approach to its logical conclusion. Even if the labeling process was the focus of the labeling approach, it still presupposed an objective act that was considered deviant according to norms that were similarly considered objective (Kitsuse and Spector, 1975: 584–5). For example, using cannabis became labeled deviant because people *were* smoking marijuana and it *was* against the norms and values of society, and therefore was later criminalized. In turn, marijuana smokers adopted a deviant identity because of the labeling and so the deviant behavior was strengthened. Most of the studies of labeling tried, after all, to explain how *persons* really – that is, in the objective sense – become deviant.

Spector and Kitsuse's radical reformulation was that deviance was important only insofar as people recognized an act as deviant. According to them, a proper sociology of social problems did not even exist (Spector and Kitsuse, 2001: 1). Spector and Kitsuse argued that for a proper sociology of social problems, the only important matter was the process whereby an act or a situation became defined as a problem, *regardless of the objective condition*. Following this line of thought, marijuana is not a social problem because some people are smoking it, but because some people are concerned about others smoking it.

Spector and Kitsuse's approach radically subjectivized the study of social problems. Their definition of social problems makes clear that objective conditions do not play any role in their study:

> Thus, we define social problems as the activities of individuals or groups making assertions of grievances and claims with respect to some putative conditions (Spector and Kitsuse, 2001: 75).

The important word here is 'putative':

> We use the word [putative] to emphasize that any given claim or complaint is about a condition *alleged* to exist, rather than about a condition that we, as sociologists are willing to verify or certify. That is, in focusing the attention to the claims-making process we set aside the question whether those claims are true or false (Spector and Kitsuse, 2001: 76; emphasis in the original).

In effect, Spector and Kitsuse take a completely disinterested stance towards any claims regarding the reality of phenomenon in question. What matters is the public reaction, and this is what sociologists should study. Therefore, the process of *claims-making* becomes the focus of constructionist study of social problems. Social problems are social movements in themselves, because the problems would not exist without people who make claims about them (Mauss, 1975). This radical approach became widely used in the study of social problems, but also ignited a critical discussion that continues to this day (see Holstein and Miller, 1993; 2003; Miller and Holstein, 1993; Best, 1995a; 2007). I will return to the question of subjectivity and objectivity and the criticisms levelled against Spector and Kitsuse's approach in Chapter 6. Now, however, I will outline the questions that the constructionist approach is interested in, namely (1) what is the content of the claims? (2) who makes claims and how are they received? and (3) what does the process of claims-making look like?

The content of social problems claims

It should be obvious from the examples above that few social problems claims convince everyone. This is because of the simple fact that we do not share a common set of values in contemporary society. The idyllic community, where everyone shares a mutual view of life and works for the good of all, does not exist today – if it ever did. Historically speaking, the fragmentation of society has not only led to an advanced division of labour and specialization, but also to a pluralism of values. In the hypercomplex societies of today, there are few things that we agree upon, the right to life and personal property being some of the basic examples. However, even in these cases, the issue becomes highly contested when we enter the discussion on abortion, or the state's right to tax.

Therefore, the construction of social problems through claims-making is a process of competition, where competing, sometimes opposing, claims vie for the position from which the reality of the social problem is primarily constructed (Williams, 1995: Loseke, 1999: 47–67). In order to do this, claims must convince audiences with argument and rhetoric. Argument and rhetoric make up what Loseke (1999: 103) calls 'packages' of social problems claims. These packages aim to show audiences why a condition is a social problem by appealing to values and constructing recognizable types of conditions and people involved in the social problem. Finally, successful social problems packages offer a solution to the problem in hand.

Values and claims competition

All social problem claims are also moral claims. When I define a condition as bad or undesirable, I am making a moral claim: this thing is wrong and something should be done about it. Again, my moral claims are based on the values that I consider important. Not everybody shares my values, of course, so in order to make my claims more effective, I have to package the claims in ways that attract the attention of those who have not previously given thought to my particular problem. I will also have to make the claims more accessible and agreeable to those who might disagree with them at first sight.

Donileen Loseke (1999: 25–6) defines a claim as 'any verbal, visual, or behavioral statement that tries to convince audiences to take a condition seriously'. The purpose of claims is to convince audiences of a particular way to think about social problems, that is, why a certain condition is undesirable or bad. Moreover, especially in the case of visual imagery, claims also attempt to affect the way that audiences feel about these problems (Loseke, 1999: 27). Whereas a rational, verbal argument may work better in demanding better educational facilities for underprivileged children in an urban Western context, a single picture of a starving African child is a much more powerful appeal to our sense of solidarity in the face of hunger in the developing world.

On the grassroots level the most important audience of claims is, of course, the people most likely to agree with the values expressed in the claims. Let's take religion, for example. The values expressed in religious texts and teachings are an important source of claims. However, even in the case of religious values, the social problems claims tend to be clothed in more broad terms outside the particular church, synagogue, temple, or mosque and its constituents. First of all, broadening the scope of claims by excluding explicitly sectarian formulations attracts concerned citizens outside one's own religious constituency. Secondly, in order to have legislative and judicial effect, claims need to have a secular argument in addition to the religious. This is the outcome of either a formal church–state separation (as in the United States) or a more culturally secularized atmosphere (as in the Nordic countries). For example, evangelical Christian claims about satanic cults in America went largely unheeded outside the evangelicals' own circle until Satanism was claimed to include systematic child abuse, a crime with identifiable victims and specific cultural shock value (Best, 2001: 3–8).

Bad conditions, victims and villains

For a social problem claim to be successful, it must address its audience with descriptions of actual conditions and people instead of abstract values. In fact, talking about values at an abstract level easily can be seen as negative, as 'just talk.' In contrast, claims-making that talks about 'the destruction of the earth's lungs' when talking about the conservation of rainforests, or 'babies killed before they are born' in the case of abortion, is sure to attract attention. Whether that attention is negative or positive depends on the receptiveness of different constituencies, but, whatever the response, public interest in the condition is aroused. In addition, successful claims-making always pinpoints the actors in the social problems drama. 'Drug dealers' and 'mass murderers' are much more effective nametags than 'illegal substance trafficking' or 'social pathology'.

The purpose of constructing conditions, victims and villains is to narrow down the complexity of social life in order to focus the social problem claim. Typification is the process where conditions and people are presented in a particular way and is crucial to the process of social problems construction: 'Claims must be typifications. There is no choice because social life is too complex' (Loseke, 1999: 101; see Chapter 2). Consider sexually transmitted diseases among teenagers: is the problematic condition 'teen promiscuity' or 'lack of sex education'? Although the problem remains the same, it makes a world of difference how it is typified. Naming is a very important way of typifying conditions and people (Best, 1995b: 7–9).

In addition to conditions, persons are also typified. 'Drug dealer' often tells people all they need to know about a person, although traffickers in illegal substances come in many varieties. Some are 'drug lords' that control large international schemes; some are people who sell small amounts of cannabis to friends, and everything in between. But hearing the word 'drug-dealer' gives us an impression of a person, regardless of the actual variety and complexity of the lives of these people. 'Drug-dealer' is a type of person we recognize (Loseke, 1999: 70–72). Similarly, the concept of 'abused children' includes a wide variety of life histories and actual types of victimization. Nevertheless, the power of the concept lies in its recognizability and the images of the victim it evokes.

An effective claim of a problematic condition must represent it as widespread and as having troublesome consequences. Furthermore, it must point out victims and responsibility. In other words, a successful social problems claim must include a condemnation of a condition and descriptions of what the condition is about, a statement of to whom the condition is deplorable, and a nomination of who is responsible. Only then can claims-makers start thinking about the question: what can be done about the social problem?

Solutions for social problems

In addition to pointing out a threat to values, and personalizing social problems by constructing convincing conditions and people, effective claims-making offers solutions to the problems posed. In fact, separating solutions claims from constructions of moralities, conditions and people is somewhat artificial, since the solution is almost always implied in the description of the problematic condition, victim, or villain (Loseke, 1999: 102). Some have also suggested that solutions actually come first:

> The striking characteristic of the link between political problems and solutions in daily life is that the solution typically comes first, chronologically and psychologically. Those who favor a particular course of governmental action are likely to cast about for a widely feared problem to which to attach it in order to maximize its support (Edelman, 1988: 22).

Whatever the actual chain of motivation is, solutions are important in the sense that they not only tell people that a condition is a social problem, but what to do about that problem. This has two main implications (Loseke, 1999: 99–100). First, the solution claims can focus on individual change. This goes for a variety of issues ranging from recycling to racism. We know that we should separate our paper trash from other trash and recycle bottles in order to save the environment. We also know that in a just society people should not categorize others because of their skin colour. We, as individuals, must change in order to solve the problems of environmental strain or racism.

There is, however, only so much we can do individually. Sometimes individuals and even communities of people do not have enough resources to fight a condition they see as problematic. In other cases people do not necessarily see a problem, where one could be legitimately constructed, or they are not willing to do anything about it. In these cases the government can intervene and offer solutions. In this second type of solution-construction, social problems become the focus of social policy. Funding more effective trash collection and giving a refund for used bottles, or by placing sanctions on unsorted household trash, may encourage recycling, not to speak about restrictions on the dumping of industrial waste. Similarly, laws and governmental initiatives may encourage more equal treatment of minorities in education and in employment, as the affirmative action and equal opportunities schemes adopted in many countries attest.

Successful construction of solutions differs from the construction of morality, conditions, and people in the sense that it has the most direct consequences on social change, which is, at the end of the day, at the heart of the claims-making competition (Loseke, 1999: 119). However, the initiatives taken in the social policy arena are especially prone to creating new kinds of problems. As an imaginary example, if the budget for the maintenance of prisons is raised, the budget for secondary education has to be cut down. This in turn creates a new type of social problem claims. In politics, the claims of the opposition are mainly based on pointing out the problems that the policies of the current government have engendered. A new round of claims begins with the opposition offering different political solutions for perceived social problems. I will return to the cycle of claims-making later, but first I will discuss the actual people behind the claims and the audiences of claims.

Claims-makers and their audiences

If and when social problems are understood as claims-making activity and a kind of social movement, the next step is to determine who are the organizations and people making the claims. Furthermore, a thorough study of the construction of social problems should also take into account the motives behind claims-making activities, that is, why people engage in claims-making. Lastly, studying only the form of claims cannot adequately assess the effect of social problems claims. The role of audiences is a crucial, but often neglected part in the study of claims-making processes.

Who makes claims?

In effect, everyone is a claims-maker. When we complain about the price of food in the supermarket queue, or wear a T-shirt that states 'Free Pussy Riot', we are making a claim about a condition that we find objectionable. It is, however, reasonable to distinguish everyday claims-making from deliberate efforts to bring about a change in conditions found objectionable. This latter type of claims-making can be called, following Donileen Loseke (1999: 29–32), the social problems industry.

There are multiple ways of categorizing claims-makers in the social problems industry (Mauss, 1975: 11–12; Loseke, 1999: 29–32; Spector and Kitsuse, 2001: 88). A very rudimentary way of discussing the various sources of claims is to differentiate between primary and secondary claims-makers – although the line between the two is not always clear. For example, politicians and political lobbyists fall quite naturally into the group of primary claims-makers. It is, after all, their job to make claims about conditions and offer solutions to these conditions. Organizations such as workers' unions, Christian associations, and a myriad of interest groups (Greenpeace, the Occupy Wall Street protesters, the local parents' association against youth drug abuse, and so on) are also primary claims-makers. Their existence is based on the effort to make a particular social problem widely recognized.

The news media is commonly given as an example of secondary claims-making. Taken at face value, the purpose of the media is to *mediate* information about conditions and activities relevant to social problems. This is, however, now commonly regarded as a naïve approach to the role of the media in modern society (Hall et al., 1978; Fairclough, 1995a; Thompson, 1995; Cohen, 2002). Instead of viewing media as a neutral, interest-free conduit, current scholarship acknowledges that the media can also be a source of claims-making in itself, thus acting as an active participant in social problems construction.[1]

Social problems claims are also a growing part of the entertainment industry. With the advent of reality TV, audiences have witnessed the proliferation of shows showing 'authentic' real-life situations dealing with issues as diverse as crime (*Cops, America's Most Wanted*) and infidelity (*Cheaters*). Immensely popular talk shows such as *Oprah* frequently use themes such as poverty, drug abuse, sexual abuse, and family problems in their repertoire. In this way, at least for a certain segment of the population, contemporary social problems are encountered mostly through entertainment television (Barak, 1994a: 22–4; Loseke, 1999: 30).

Why are claims made?

Although many, if not most, social problems claims are made in the name of an organization, there are always real people behind the claims. Organizations established to combat social problems would not exist in the first place without the motivation of individuals. Concurrently, it is not sufficient to categorize different claims-makers solely according to their organizational status and their position in society. What is also needed is a model that describes the different motives behind social problems activity and helps to explain the dynamics of social problems construction.

Again, there are multiple choices as to how to categorize different reasons for becoming a social problems activist (see Mauss, 1975: 14–19; Loseke, 1999: 32–4; Spector and Kitsuse. 2001: 88). The most comprehensive of these models is the one introduced by Erich Goode and Nachman Ben-Yehuda in their book *Moral Panics* (1994). The types of claims-making motivation can be grouped into different 'cells' (see Table 3.1) depending on whether the social problem has been constructed because a condition is found morally objectionable or if there have been material or status interests involved. This motivational dimension is compared to the social level at which the social problems activities – that is, claims-making – takes place. The levels are divided into elite, middle, and public. Basically, the main function of these categories is to show how many people are involved in claims-making. Further, they also indicate the level of social power that the claims-makers have (Goode and Ben-Yehuda, 1994: 124–5).

Table 3.1   Typology of the motives and origins of social problems claims (adapted from Goode and Ben-Yehuda, 1994: 125)

	Morality/Ideology	Material/Status Interests
Elite	A	B
Middle	C	D
Public	E	F

Regarding the motivational dimension, it is, of course, impossible to completely separate moral or ideological motives from interests, as they frequently overlap. It is equally difficult to define what constitutes the different levels. Elites are commonly regarded as the segment of society that has most institutional and financial power. That includes, for example, corporate executives and political and military leaders. National and international media organizations can be also included in this level. The 'middle' level includes people and organizations with considerably less power, both economic and institutional. Local media, local law enforcement, social movements and smaller lobby groups can be included in this category. The 'public' or the grassroots level is everyone else who does not have significant institutional authority or access to major financial resources (Goode and Ben-Yehuda, 1994: 125).

Now, comparing the motivational dimension and the social level, we can see that not all of the 'cells' in Goode and Ben-Yehuda's model are equally probable empirically. For example, cases where claims are made on the basis of elite ideology (cell A) alone seem unlikely. As Goode and Ben-Yehuda (1994: 125–6) remind us, 'in western society, profoundly influenced as we are by Marxist thinking, it is difficult for us to imagine ideology divorced from elite interests'. Even if cases like the Iranian revolution of 1979 could be said to represent instances of cell A (opposition to a secular regime by religiously motivated Muslim leaders), this type of social problem construction remains rare. The argument that grassroots-level claims are made primarily out of material or status interests (cell F) also has few or no proponents (Goode and Ben-Yehuda, 1994: 127). But again, it is important to remember that, although morality and material interests are separable in theory, they are difficult to distinguish in most cases: 'Advancing a moral and ideological cause almost inevitably entails advancing the status (and often also the material interests) of the group who believes in it, and advancing the status and material interests of a group may simultaneously advance its morality and ideology' (Goode and Ben-Yehuda, 1994: 139). Therefore, especially historically speaking, the workers' movement protests, and poor people taking to the streets, could be well said to represent a situation where the grassroots is mobilized because of material interests. Yet, mobilization of that kind is almost certainly motivated by an outrage at inequality – that is, a moral claim.

The traditional Marxist version of the construction of social problems can be found in cell B. According to this argument, elites 'engineer' social problems in order to further their material or status interests. Perhaps the most famous study made from this perspective is Stuart Hall et al.'s *Policing the Crisis* (1978), which argues that the wave of fear related to mugging that struck Britain in the early 1970s was instigated by political elites that tried to divert attention from the ineffectiveness of the political system by directing public consideration to street crime (Hall et al., 1978). In addition to Hall et al. and studies inspired by their landmark book, a branch of criminology referred to as 'newsmaking criminology' also employs a broadly Marxist approach to crime, and especially the public representation of crime (Barak, 1994b; Fishman, 1998).

Arguments that emphasize the social movement nature of social problems (especially Mauss, 1975 and Blumer, 1971) fall into cells C and D. These interpretations are commonly referred to as interest-group theory (Goode and Ben-Yehuda, 1994: 138–141). In *The Outsiders* (1991[1963]), Howard Becker introduced the concept of 'moral entrepreneurs' that he used to denote people who make the rules that define certain acts as deviant (Becker, 1991: 147–63). These can be law enforcement personnel worried about youth crime (Zatz, 1987), religious groups alarmed by the rise of 'the occult' in contemporary culture (Victor, 1989; 1993), social service workers concerned about threats to children (Jenkins, 1992; LaFontaine, 1998), and so on. Social movement theories of social problems (cells C and D) are often treated together because, again, in practice it is difficult to separate between moral–ideological and material interests.

Lastly, there is the grass-roots approach to the creation of social problems (cell E). Perspectives that favour the grass-roots theory claim that even if politicians and the media are often the ones that bring a social problem into public awareness, their actions are always a reflection of a more widespread concern among the 'masses' (Goode and Ben-Yehuda, 1994: 127). One of the most interesting contributions to this approach is Kai T. Erikson's book *Wayward Puritans* (1966), in which he combines historical data from seventeenth-century Massachusetts with sociological theories of deviance. Erikson argues that by 'finding' deviance in Quakers or presumed witches, the Puritan community actually upheld their solidarity. The rules and moralities – the boundaries – of the community were strengthened by the process of pointing out evil inside the community. This often happens in a time of crisis, which does not have to be related in any way to the fears of the community (Erikson, 1966: 64). For example, the Massachusetts Puritans were living in a utopia with few precedents and in which the boundaries were continually being shaped and reshaped. Making clear what the community was *not* could alleviate the consequent identity crisis.

In his argument, Erikson is closely following the propositions Émile Durkheim presented in his *Division of Labour in Society* (1984 [1893]). Of course, in the case of the Massachusetts Puritans, there were certain key figures that instigated the sentiments of the population and made the persecutions possible. However, the point that Erikson (following Durkheim) makes is that society needs deviance and social problems in order to be able to draw the boundaries of what is acceptable and what is not – and this can happen effectively only if the grassroots level is involved.

The audiences of claims

Goode and Ben-Yehuda's model is helpful in typifying ways in which social problem claims are generated. At the same time, many studies of social problems construction pay less attention to the reception of claims, that is, they often lack an explicit focus on the role of audiences (Loseke, 1999: 37, 59; cf. Mauss, 1975: 11–12).

Even if we can conclude that a certain social problem has the support of a broad grass-roots constituency, the claims do not reach – not to mention convince – *everyone* even in a small tightly knit community. Neither does a social problem claim made by the prime minister or the president convince everyone. This could be readily seen in the mixed reactions towards the claims that the governments of the United States and the United Kingdom used to legitimate the war in Iraq.

The key word here is 'audiences', not 'audience' (Loseke, 1999: 37). Even if concepts such as 'The American public' or 'The British public' are used in popular discourse, claims very rarely touch all the levels of society in the same way. It should be remembered that the context is the key to understanding why social problems succeed or fail: Some audiences are not receptive to some problems, and some audiences are too busy thinking about other problems. Therefore, no matter how efficient from an organizational point of view, claims may only succeed if they are targeted right. The same problem may have to be clothed in different terms for different audiences, even if the bottom line remains the same (cf. Loseke, 1999: 42n5).

Firstly, for a social problem to exist, it has to be recognized as such by the audiences. Claims are 'a common-sense category, understood by members of a society and often associated with terms such as demands, complaints, gripes, and requests' (Spector and Kitsuse, 2001: 79). As simple as this might sound, not all claims are even recognized as such. While we may hear and see the politicians, social movement activists, and news media people making claims, we might not listen or watch what they are actually saying (Loseke, 1999: 38). For the proverbial middle-class housewife who spends her days taking care of the household and watching television soap operas, the news about inner-city poverty might not even look like social problem claims. It just does not concern her in any way.

Secondly, audiences have to care about the content of the claims. The proverbial middle-class housewife's concern over inner-city poverty might be aroused only if the problems somehow affected her own neighbourhood. In the field of politics the 'provincial proneness' to particular social problems claims is institutionalized in countries that have a multi-party system.

Alongside major parties that (claim to) represent wider interests, these countries often have political parties that represent certain specific language groups, religious groups, age groups, and so on. These parties often remain small and marginal, exactly because their political claims are relevant mostly to the constituency they are established to address.

Thirdly, audiences differ in power. If a claims-maker is successful in convincing, say, the local government of the need for new roads, it is not necessary to convince everyone living in the areas affected by the prospective roadwork. Unless all the people affected by the decision unite in active opposition against it, the claims-makers need only to convince the people who have the power to make a decision regarding the roads. Knowing how to find audiences who are interested in the claim and who have the power to change the condition implicated in the claim is the main task of claims-makers.

The 'natural history' of social problems

An important element of all constructionist approaches to social problems is the emphasis on the process nature of problem construction. This process is often outlined in a model referred to as the 'natural history' of social problems. The perhaps surprising choice of words – from a constructionist perspective, the idea of something having a 'natural', predetermined history sounds problematic – is meant to denote the recurring characteristics observable in many social problems. A particular social problem has a history, but 'natural histories […] are based on sequences of events common to the histories of particular cases whether they are persons or institutions' (Spector and Kitsuse, 2001: 137). In other words, natural histories are sociological abstractions of empirical processes. Although used widely in the earlier discussions of social problems (Fuller and Myers, 1941; Lemert, 1967; Blumer, 1971; Mauss, 1975), the concept of natural history was at some point replaced by the term *career* that reflects the same process nature of social problems (Becker, 1991; see Hjelm, 2008). However, since 'career' can refer both to individual biography and patterns of social action, it is useful to retain the concept of natural history that refers explicitly to the latter.

There are several different formulations of the natural history model,[2] most of which are improvements of the original presented by Fuller and Myers in their 1941 article quoted above. I have chosen to describe the one outlined by Armand Mauss (1975: 61–8), because I think it offers the clearest analysis of the natural history process in simple categories. Mauss divides the process of social problem construction into five stages: (1) incipiency, (2) coalescence, (3) institutionalization, (4) fragmentation, and (5) demise.

As noted above, from a constructionist perspective 'a social problem does not exist unless it is recognized by the society to exist' (Blumer, 1971:302). A social problem in its incipient stage consists of a 'concerned public' (Mauss, 1975: 61) that perceives a certain condition to be threatening to its values, interests, the harmonious continuation of everyday life, and so on. In order to change this condition, the distressed public, which at this stage is unorganized and uncoordinated, seeks to focus attention on the condition and raise general awareness of the situation (Fuller and Myers, 1941: 322–4). On the 'grass-roots' level this may include gathering information on the particular condition, writing letters to the editor and to government representatives, and holding *ad hoc* meetings (Mauss, 1975: 61–2). In some cases, even violence may be used to bring attention to a particular problem (Blumer, 1971: 302; Mauss, 1975: 202–3). Many of the 'crime watch' or 'neighbourhood watch' groups – assuming that they have not been initiated by local law enforcement officials – start out as uncoordinated attempts of residents to put a stop to a perceived increase in crime and consequent insecurity (see Franz and Warren, 1987; Portney and Berry, 1997; cf. Sasson, 1995: 185–6; Putnam, 2000: 312–18).

The second stage, coalescence, is characterized by the formation of the leadership and active membership base. An organizational structure, although not fully realized yet, will be outlined and the establishment of local chapters is encouraged. In the mass media, the proponents begin to be seen as comprising a distinct movement. Also, although not yet fully organized, the movement is difficult to repress without extensive measures. For example, the contemporary movements whose aim is to raise awareness of inequality and other downsides stemming from economic globalization are commonly regarded as a global movement, although a lot of the activities are unorganized and the movement lacks a common organizational framework.

The period of institutionalization marks the heyday of a social problem movement. With institutionalization, the modest beginnings acquire 'all the characteristics of a "full blown" movement' (Mauss, 1975: 63) including:

> [S]ociety-wide organization and coordination (unless the movement happens to deal with strictly local issues); a large base of members and resources; an extended division of labor; regular thrusts into the political processes of the society (e.g. lobbying, campaigning in elections); and growing respectability (Mauss, 1975: 63).

Many of today's globally recognized social (problem) movements such as Greenpeace and Amnesty International have become institutionalized to the point where even governments that are recurrently criticized by the same groups have to take their complaints into account. This is rarely done in a straightforward manner, but the public pressure that the movements create often has indirect effects when upholding the respectability of governments becomes too costly in the face of public discontent. An example of an institutionalized social problem movement that has had a direct effect on legislation and the general political and cultural climate is the civil rights movement in the United States. Laws against discrimination and initiatives such as affirmative action and equal opportunity had their beginning in the more grass-roots movement of the 1950s and 1960s but are now institutionalized in civil rights lobbying and co-optation by the government itself (Mauss, 1975: 543–8).

The success of institutionalization has, however, its downside. Ironically, in most cases the institutionalization of a social problem movement and its programme has a divisive effect that leads to the fragmentation of the movement. First, some grass-roots supporters may find that with institutionalization the problem has been solved and turn their interests to other causes. Second, institutionalized movements often develop – both explicitly and implicitly – a hierarchical system of membership, in which some members holding 'radical' views are relegated to the margins, creating tension within the movement regarding the 'proper' way of addressing the agenda. Third, the terms of leadership may become contested, leading to a process where the original membership is divided according to boundaries drawn by different leadership opinions (Mauss, 1975: 64–5). In a way, fragmentation marks the birth of a 'second-generation' social problem with the 'development of activities to create alternative, parallel, or counter-institutions as responses to the established procedures' (Spector and Kitsuse, 2001: 142).

Eventually, most social problems die. It is – again – somewhat ironic that the realization of the objectives of a social problem movement also marks its demise. This is not the only way in which social problems are 'forgotten', but interestingly enough, if a social problem movement aspires to sustain its influence, it has to continually refocus its claims to adjust to a situation in which at least some of its demands have been met. In the United States the prohibitionist movement of the late nineteenth and early twentieth century declined after the imposition of Prohibition in 1920. However, the demise need not be complete. Either the social problem movement is revived from the struggling remains of an existing movement, or a new movement with a similar agenda and similar goals replaces the old one, continuing its 'heritage' in intent, if not in organization (Mauss, 1975: 67–8). Many differences notwithstanding, the affinity of the contemporary anti-alcoholism movement with the early prohibitionists suggests just such a development (Mauss, 1975: 312; see Gusfield, 1986; Tracy and Acker, 2004).

It is important to remember that the natural history cycle of a social problem always occurs in interaction with the host society, and often independently of objective conditions. A social problem disappears when the perceptions of it have changed enough to warrant the demise of an effective social problem movement, regardless of the actual social conditions (Mauss, 1975: 66). Therefore, the 'naturalness' of the natural history of a social problem is indeed in the eye of the beholder.

Case study: Constructing crime

I have mentioned many potential social problems in the preceding sections. Now I would like to take a brief look at one specific instance constructing social problems, namely the construction of crime. Crime is a good example, because everyone knows, at least intuitively, what the term means, and the very definition of crime itself lends to an understanding that it is a social problem. Criminologists Gary Potter and Victor Kappeler are not exaggerating when they note that

> There is probably no issue that more consistently, over a longer period and with greater emotion, influences public opinion than crime. The results of poll after poll demonstrate that crime – in general or a specific crime issue – captures public attention. Whether the issue is drug-related crime, violent crime, juvenile crime, child abductions, serial killers, youth gangs, or crime against the elderly, a public consensus exists that crime is rampant, dangerous, and threatening to explode. The dangers of crime are seen as immediate, omnipresent, and almost inescapable (Potter and Kappeler, 1998: 1).

Although Potter and Kappeler are referring specifically to the American situation, the same sentiment rings true in most societies. Crime seems to be an ever-present and unavoidable fact of modern life. That being said, as the constructionist perspective once again shows, our everyday notions of things are rarely as simple as we would like to believe.

What is crime?

Most people have quite a clear understanding of what crime is. In its simplest form, crime is conceived as an act that is against the law. But where does law come from? It would not be a great exaggeration to say that most people also do not question the validity or the origin of social definitions of law and crime. In other words, the understanding of what crime *is* is often reified, concealing its constructed nature. However, a few very simple examples show that crime is, in fact, a social construction *par excellence*.

Consider the wide variation in definitions of crime between different cultures. In Iran, for example, homosexuality is a crime, and homosexual acts are punishable by death, in the worst case. In stark contrast, most European states have laws regulating against the discrimination of sexual minorities. It is clear that even if there are people condemning homosexuality in both contexts, the law, and thus crime, is differently constructed.

But the question is not only about cultural differences. Changing definitions of crime on the temporal axis also show that crime is not a static concept. Four hundred years ago condemning people to death for witchcraft was a common phenomenon in some parts of Europe, whereas it would seem very out of place to punish people for practicing witchcraft in the contemporary world. In fact, the situation has turned on its head in the sense that the right to practice witchcraft is protected by law, to the extent that it does not violate any other laws.

The definition of crime differs not only on the level of law making. The actual enforcement of laws can differ markedly even within one particular society. If public opinion does not support strict enforcement, some types of crime can pass relatively unhindered as a consequence of more lax enforcement, as is the case with public drinking laws, or even narcotic laws in the case of 'soft drugs' in some European urban areas. The extent of enforcement affects the public's behaviour much more than the 'letter of the law': '[W]e are influenced much less by the posted speed limit than by our estimates of actual police enforcement practices' (Mauss, 1975: 77).

Added to all that has been said above, the actual rate of crime is notoriously difficult to assess. This is partly so because many crimes go unreported and undetected, partly because of varying statistical measures used in gathering information about crime. Therefore, what passes as crime in society can never be accurately described in a strictly objective sense. What can be assessed and sometimes even sensed in the general cultural atmosphere, however, is the concern over crime.

Concern over crime

Émile Durkheim's famous thesis – which was in stark contrast with the common understanding of the issue in his time – was that crime was a necessary component of society (Durkheim, 1984). In a Durkheim-inspired statement, Kai T. Erikson neatly summarizes this perspective: 'One of the surest ways to confirm an identity, for communities as well as for individuals, is to find some way of measuring what one is *not*' (Erikson, 1966: 64; emphasis in the original). Therefore, from a Durkheimian perspective, crime, and especially the concern over crime, is an unavoidable feature of social life. Communities need the 'bad guy' in order to maintain the boundaries of acceptable behaviour. But how do we learn about crime? How do we recognize it for what it is and how do we come to consider certain types of crime more relevant than others?

First, it is possible that we have experienced crime ourselves. This is quite straightforward. However, only a small percentage of the population of any country has been directly affected by crime and, ironically, it is often those that have no direct experience of crime that are most worried about it (Mauss, 1975: 89; cf. Chiricos, Eschholz and Gertz, 1998). Therefore, personal experience accounts only for a small proportion of the ideas about crime.

Second, a much more important factor is the image of crime that people internalize in socialization. Almost everybody has a story about a neighbour's friend that got mugged, or a friend of a friend whose house was broken into. These crime narratives form a social reservoir of 'common sense' about crime in a particular social context. In almost every major urban area there is a neighbourhood that is considered dangerous at night. Sometimes this is indeed the case, but whatever the reality, the 'knowledge' is rarely based on statistical information, for example, but rather on word of mouth talk and 'streetwise' learned in social interaction.

Third, with the advent of the mass media, especially television, most of our knowledge of crime comes from the news and increasingly from 'true crime' type entertainment (Barak, 1994a; Potter and Kappeler, 1998: 3). Sometimes the media information can be in conflict with the experiences and shared knowledge of a community. Therefore, it is too simplistic to say that crime news and entertainment dictate peoples' opinions on crime in any direct sense (see Gans, 1993; Sacco, 1995). First of all, crime news competes with (and often loses to) sports, daytime soap operas, and so on. However, media representations of crime affect the popular image of crime indirectly: even if you missed last night's news, your neighbour might have seen it. She in turn tells you about the rising number of cases of violent crime in your neighbourhood. The power of the media lies in shaping the topics of discussion, not necessarily in telling us what to think about crime.

If crime is – as it seems to be – continuously represented as the main topic in news, it is bound to have an effect on the image that people have about the *amount* of crime. As expressed in the above quote by Potter and Kappeler, as an effect of the contemporary media fixation the 'dangers of crime are seen as immediate, omnipresent, and almost inescapable' (Potter and Kappeler, 1998: 1). In addition to the amount of crime, media images also shape the concern over particular *types* of crime. Media accounts of crime overwhelmingly focus on so-called 'predatory' crimes, such as robbery and violence. These crimes have an identifiable victim and often also an identifiable perpetrator. If the media is full of stories of 'street crime', we are more likely to talk about that than cases of fraud and other 'white-collar' crime that are much less publicized and differently reported (Lofquist, 1998; Sacco, 1995). As pointed out at the beginning of the chapter, successful claims need identifiable conditions and victims. And the more the audiences can relate to crime news, the more tangible effects the public 'crime talk' has.

Public perceptions of the amount and type of crime are often in stark contrast to the social-scientific knowledge about crime. Of course, if one wants to follow a 'strict' or relativist interpretation of constructionism (see Chapter 6), the actual difference between social-scientific or statistical knowledge about crime and the public fear of crime is irrelevant. After all, what counts is the claims-making process (Spector and Kitsuse, 2001: 76). However, the perception of crime becomes interesting when we begin to assess the effects of crime images.

The effects of crime images

The effects of crime images, especially those represented in the media, are notoriously difficult to assess. The debate on media effects has raged ever since the early twentieth century, without a consensus on the most valid approach (Scheufele and Tewksbury, 2007). However, although more empirical research needs to be done on the issue, some general effects can be briefly outlined.

First, as mentioned above, the most visible effect of 'crime talk' – both in face-to-face interaction and mediated form – is the generation of an atmosphere of fear. A look at the British government's *Crime in England and Wales* survey of 2010/11 demonstrate the discrepancy between the concern over crime and the actual experience of crime. The study shows that 2.6 per cent of households in England and Wales were victims of burglary once or more and 3.1 per cent of adults were victims of violent crime once or more. However, for each of these crimes 13 per cent of adults were 'very worried' about becoming a victim.[3]

Fear of personal safety can have wide-ranging consequences if it takes over an individual. On the other hand, talking about crime can help in getting a balanced view of actual crime; but if one is dependent on the media, especially the sensationalist entertainment media, the picture that one constructs can increase the sense of fear and have an effect in personal behaviour, ranging from isolation to potential gun use for self-protection. Whether the fear of crime is based on 'facts' or is a 'thing of the mind', it has real consequences (Fishman, 1998: 53; Smolej and Kivivuori, 2006).

Second, in the media-driven environment of contemporary societies, public policy is heavily influenced by media images. Social issues that get prime-time coverage on national television are much more probable to attract the attention of policy makers than issues that are not featured in the media. Political responses to the 'crack attack' and the notion of 'war on drugs' in the USA in the 1980s (Reinarman and Levine, 1995; Chermak, 1998) were heavily influenced by the attention that the media gave to the issue – especially when compared to other types of crime that never ceased to exist but which were relegated to a secondary status in the attempt to eradicate drugs from the market. The 'real effects' of the media panic, if you will (Jenkins, 1998), were that law enforcement resources were directed to combat drug manufacture, distribution and use, at the same time taking away resources from other areas of crime control.

Third, looking at the issue from a slightly different angle, crime talk can actually contribute to certain types of crime. This happens when a person is labelled as a 'junkie' 'car thief', or what have you. Through a process of *secondary deviation* (Lemert, 1967) the person actually internalizes the label given to her from the outside and starts to act according to role expectations. For example, even if a person's drug use does not affect his or her performance at work, getting labelled as an addict will probably get the person fired. This in turn may force the person 'into other illegitimate kinds of activity, such as robbery and theft, by the refusal of respectable employers to have him around' (Becker, 1991: 34). When this experience is repeated often enough, the problems created by the social reaction to the drug use 'become central facts of existence for those experiencing them, altering psychic structure, [and] producing specialized organization of social roles and self-regarding attitudes' (Lemert, 1967: 40–41). Having been thrust to the margins of 'respectable' society the labelled person becomes socialized into the deviant role. In this way, a vicious circle of definitions and behaviour is created.

In conclusion, constructions of crime – regardless of their truth value – have tangible effects on social life. Fear, public policy and sometimes actual criminal behaviour are shaped by our shared 'common knowledge' views of crime. The role of the constructionist approach to crime is to analyse the process where particular depictions become prevalent, and sometimes unquestioned, ways of understanding crime.

Conclusion

In this chapter I have discussed the constructionist approach to social problems. The key question is: why do some issues become widely regarded as social problems at the same time as some other, possibly equally or more harmful, issues do not? Also, how do we explain the differences in conceptions of crime in different societies and different times? We don't burn witches any more, yet it was only in 1967 that interracial marriage was legalized on the federal level in the United States. The constructionist approach to social problems sees *claims-making* as the key to understanding the emergence of social problems. In other words social problems are social movements in themselves, created by people that perceive a condition as harmful. Claims-makers, who can be government officials, interest groups, or grassroots social movements, need to create awareness of the problematic condition, name the victims and villains, and offer solutions to the problems. If successful, social problems regularly go through a process referred to as the 'natural history' of a social problem: from incipiency through coalescence and institutionalization to eventual fragmentation and demise. Crime is a specific type of social problem usually high on people's list of recognized social problems. In the case study I discussed how the fear of crime is constructed, especially in the contemporary mass media. This fear, although a 'thing of the mind', has very real consequences for individuals and societies alike.

Constructing the Self: Social Psychology, Discourse and Postmodernism

4

If you walk into any decent-sized bookshop you'll find a section on 'self-help'. There you'll find books on how to find friends and love, how to find a job, how to be confident, how to be happy, and a myriad of 'inspirational' autobiographies by celebrities and self-help experts. While this kind of literature reflects Western society and values, it is a globalizing trend. The Dr Phils of the world are available on satellite and online anywhere.

Many social scientists would agree that the success of the self-help genre is a reflection of our obsession with the individual. Modernity 'destroys' tradition (Giddens, 1994: 91), and we are less bound by the identities we are born into, such as family, profession, religion, or other qualities that positioned people in more traditional societies. Recent years have witnessed an emergence of various 'identity movements' (sexual, ethnic, religious, and so on), but people join them because they *choose to*, not because these identities have been *ascribed* to them. It is an individual choice.

To put it crudely, in the social sciences the individual has traditionally been the domain of psychology, communities the domain of sociology. While Sigmund Freud was analysing his patients in Vienna, Emile Durkheim was preparing his grand theories of society in Paris. Although their work touched upon similar issues, the division into separate domains became frozen with the institutionalization of the disciplines as academic subjects. Interestingly, it is psychology, not sociology, which has had more cultural influence and has become the main lens through which human behaviour is seen in everyday thinking. This is reflected in the success of abovementioned self-help literature and such popular science magazines as *Psychology Today* and *Psychologies*, whereas titles like *Sociology Today* or *Sociologies* are nowhere to be found – and would not probably be a very profitable business. Why? First, unlike sociology, psychology has from its beginnings represented itself as a 'hard' scientific discipline, modelling itself after the natural sciences and using the methods of experimentation and statistical analysis (Lock and Strong, 2010: 295). The more removed from everyday experience the discipline, the more authoritative its claims. Second, bluntly, it is the self that sells.

In the academic world, however, the division between psychology and sociology started to break down when thinkers on both sides of the divide began to treat the separation into the individual and social realms as an inadequate way of looking at both people and society. In sociology, thinkers inspired by Weber (including Berger and Luckmann) became more sensitive to the individual perspective, whereas in psychology the subdiscipline of social psychology was developed to accommodate the deficiency in traditional psychology regarding human interaction.

It is not my intention – and as a sociologist I would hardly be qualified – to go into a full-fledged history of psychology. For our purposes, the focus here will be on a branch of social psychology that has been called *narrative psychology* or *discursive psychology* (Potter and Wetherell, 1987; Edwards and Potter, 1992; Gergen, 1994; Gergen and Gergen, 2008: 173–180). I will use the terms interchangeably, although subtle differences between them exist. Sometimes 'discourse analysis' is also used to describe the whole subdivision of psychological research, but it is important to repeat Edwards and Potter's (1992: 11) note that 'discourse analysis' has the unfortunate consequence of sounding like just another research technique when there is much more than methodological rethinking going on. As we will see below, discursive psychology is in many ways a radical departure from the theoretical ideas of traditional psychology. It is these new formulations of the self as a social being that is of most relevance to the study of constructionisms. There is, however, a caveat to be made at this point.

Of all the chapters in this book, this one has proved to be the most difficult to find a title for. It focuses on perspectives on social constructionism that have originated within the discipline of social psychology. Specifically, I wanted to use constructionist social psychology as an example of a more 'postmodern' approach to social theory. However, constructionist social psychology is much less firmly defined as a field than the constructionist study of social problems, not to mention that the perspectives described in Chapters 2 (Berger and Luckmann) and 5 (Fairclough) rely on only one or a few theorists (see Gergen and Gergen, 2008: 173–180). Therefore, whenever I am referring to 'discursive psychology' I am doing so with full understanding that my take on the field is a selective one. Finally, while the excursion into gender in this chapter is identifiably postmodern, 'postmodern feminism' has not been simply a social psychological, but a philosophical, sociological, etc. endeavour (Tong, 1989: 217–33). However, it is fitting to include those discussions in this chapter because discursive psychology and postmodern feminism share many theoretical – namely 'constructionist' – underpinnings.

There are several issues and themes that weave together a more or less coherent whole that – while being diverse within – differs from the other perspectives discussed in this book. First, in addition to critiquing the view of language as a reflection of external reality, discursive psychology has very much identified itself in opposition to views prevailing in cognitive psychology, where the attitudes and behaviour of individuals are seen as reflections of mental processes. Second, the focus of discursive psychology is on the *self*, that is, the individual and his or her identity, but as understood through the critique of cognitive psychology. Finally, social psychological constructionism and discursive psychology have, perhaps more than any of the other perspectives discussed in this book, been identified with postmodernism. Although 'postmodernism' should be considered a broad intellectual current, some particularly postmodern ideas have had an important impact on social psychological constructionism.

The critique of representation

A significant amount of social constructionist work has risen from critique (Weinberg, 2008: 15; Gergen, 2001: 44–61). For Berger and Luckmann it was critique of the functionalist sociology of Talcott Parsons; for constructionist sociology of social problems it was dissatisfaction with the prevailing models of understanding deviance. The development of discourse analysis and discursive psychology is also to a large extent a reaction to paradigmatic – namely, cognitive – ways of understanding the object of psychology. In a broader sense, discursive psychology builds on the critique of representation.

Jonathan Potter (1996: 97–8) uses the metaphor of a mirror to discuss the traditional way of describing the world. According to this view, when we – whether in everyday conversation or in scientific discourse – describe events and things, the language we use *reflects* how things 'really' are. Potter then goes on to offer an alternative metaphor: the construction yard, which, as you will have guessed by now, treats descriptions as active *constructions* of the world. Before moving on to the positive contributions that discourse analysis has to offer, it's important to discuss the two sides of this critique of representation in more detail.

Potter's above critique is of the more common variety, where the factuality of descriptions of things 'out there' is questioned. This line of argument has illustrious precursors, especially in philosophy and sociology. Both Kuhn's idea of paradigms and Garfinkel's ethnomethodology were based on a critique of the taken-for-granted nature of 'facts'. This could be called the *critique of external representation*. Thus, language is not a passive vehicle through which the world is described, but actively contributes to our understanding of that world. This idea, of course, is at the heart of all constructionist thinking, although, as we will see later, some constructionists grant at least some independence to things outside language.

There is also a second line of critique that focuses on the prevalent ways of understanding representation in psychology. This *critique of internal representation* is the source of the development of contemporary discursive psychology and takes issue with the cognitive tradition prevalent in much of contemporary psychology. In cognitivism – and this is necessarily a rough outline – the mind is seen as a sort of processor through which our understandings of the world and ourselves are filtered. So, when people react hostilely to, say, an insult directed at them, cognitive psychologists see the hostility as an outcome of mental processes. Central areas of cognitivist inquiry, such as attitudes (Potter and Wetherell, 1987) memories, and attribution (representations of causes and reasons for action; Edwards and Potter, 1992) have all become targets of constructionist and discursive critique.

For our purposes, the important point about the critique of cognitive psychology is the necessary shift in focus that a constructionist or discursive approach entails. Edwards and Potter (1992: 15–18) put this succinctly by stating that we should treat discourse as a topic in itself instead of a pathway to cognition:

> [C]onversational remembering ceases to be of interest merely because it might be a route to underlying cognitive processes; rather the organization and functions of such talk become the issue. [...] [T]opicalizing discourse, rather than using it as a pathway to memories and attributions, cuts across the conventional (although still controversial) pigeon-holing of cognitive psychology to reveal a quite different order of process at work (Edwards and Potter, 1992: 16).

This move is similar to the developments in sociology that we explored earlier, but the target is different. Where constructionist sociology questioned the determining effects of social structure, constructionist psychology turns the attention inwards, questioning the determining effects of cognitive processes. A focus on discourse as *action* draws our attention to what is being *done* with discourse, rather than how attitudes – conceived as mental properties – are reflected in discourse. This is the 'function' of discourse discussed in Chapter 1.

The critique of internal representation and the action orientation of discourse have had a significant impact on one the key areas of psychology, namely the study of 'the person' and personality. Whereas traditional (cognitive) psychology has conceived the person to be a reflection of the properties of the mind, the discursive approach argues that being a person is an interactional (or interdiscursive) achievement.

The person, identity and discourse

The idea of the self as an individual is, historically speaking, a relatively recent invention. Looking back to the roots of Western civilization, thinkers such as Aristotle, for example, did not differentiate between the individual and society in the sense that we nowadays do. Although deeply embedded in collective tradition by our modern standards, the centuries after Aristotle witnessed a gradual emergence of the idea of an individual as the primary unit of social interchange. Descartes' famous dictum 'I think, therefore I am' (*cogito ergo sum*) gave the idea of the self a philosophical and epistemological grounding, and Western culture has never been the same after this idea started to be applied in everyday life during the Enlightenment in the seventeenth and eighteenth centuries (see Lock and Strong, 2010: 226–7). To put it somewhat crudely, as the outcome of this transformation people changed from being cogs in the machine of society into independent 'machines' without which the idea of society would be unthinkable.[1] Social action became thought of as the outcome of individual minds rather than collective norms and roles. According to this view, we have an essential 'self' that is our 'personality', something that we possess as individuals. Needless to say, this view has been most pronounced in psychology, the remit of which has always been to study the individual mind or the 'psyche'.

The idea of the individual person, or the 'personality' of people, as something discoverable by scientific psychological method was challenged from the 1970s onward by what later became known as the social constructionist movement in modern psychology (Gergen, 1985). People like Kenneth Gergen (1991) and John Shotter (1993) in the USA, and Jonathan Potter (1996) and Margaret Wetherell (Potter and Wetherell, 1987) in the UK, critiqued the individualist agenda of psychology and called for a refocusing of the field, arguing that individuals are not made of the mental processes inside their heads, but rather by interactions with other people and by the ways in which people communicate in and about those interactions. Gergen (1994: 185) provides us with a formative statement:

> I want to propose a relational view of self-conception, one that views self-conception not as an individual's personal and private cognitive structure but as *discourse* about the self – the performance of languages available in the public sphere. I replace the traditional concern with conceptual strategies (self-concepts, schemas, self-esteem), with the self as a narration rendered intelligible within ongoing relationships. (Emphasis in the original.)

In other words, being 'a person' is not an individual achievement, but rather a *relational* process of becoming. Gergen (and others) illustrate this by showing how we are different in different social contexts. We talk differently to our grandparents at a Christmas dinner than we do to friends while clubbing on the weekend. While this in itself is not very revelatory, the point Gergen makes is that this is the way we make sense of others, of the world more broadly, but also of ourselves. There is no stable personality to be discovered beyond the narratives and discourses we use to account for ourselves. The stability of our 'personality' is, from a constructionist perspective, in fact another 'story' or discourse we tell ourselves and others in order to make life comprehensible (e.g. Shotter, 1993: 44; Gergen, 1994: 186). In fact, our ways of speaking about 'personality' belie its relational character. Consider words like 'friendly', 'caring', 'shy' and 'charming' – all common characterizations of 'personality'. Then consider what they would mean to a lone person on the proverbial desert island. Does 'charming' make sense without a relationship to another person? It would need a stretch of the imagination for it to do so (see Burr, 1995: 27).

This step from an individual's mind to a relational conception of the self has led to a change in the vocabulary of constructionist psychology. Instead of 'personality', the individual 'psyche' or mental 'schemas', discursive psychologists prefer to talk about *identity*. Identity 'avoids the essentialist connotations of personality, and is also an implicitly social concept. As Berger and Luckmann (and others, see Chapter 2) suggest, our identity is formed in our social interactions. But discursive psychology, more so than any other form of constructionism, wants to do away with any lingering ideas about a 'core' personality that exists beyond interaction and our discourse about interaction. It is a position that can be difficult to accept from a 'commonsense' point of view. That is how deeply ingrained the ideas about an inner personality are to our modern culture. I will illustrate this constructionist alternative with an excursion into ideas about gender and identity, but before that we need to discuss the postmodernist thought that is an important source of the critique of essentialism in psychology.

Postmodernism and social constructionism

In a recent assessment of constructionism, Dave Elder-Vass (2012: 4) bluntly states that 'in the twenty-first century postmodernism [...] is dead'. While sympathies seem to have indeed shifted even within the decade or so that I have been interested in constructionism, the legacy of postmodernism – as Elder-Vass also notes – still lingers. Although in no way exclusively a phenomenon in social psychology, postmodernist ideas have been more pronounced in discursive psychology than any of the other constructionisms examined in this book (especially Shotter, 1993; Gergen, 1994). While Potter (1996: 88) warns that defining postmodernism might not be wise to begin with, its prevalence in social psychological constructionism makes it appropriate to briefly discuss its main impact here.

Although not mentioned in the previous section on the 'self', views such as Gergen's are explicitly grounded in postmodern thought. Hence,

[u]nder postmodern conditions, persons exist in a state of continuous construction and reconstruction; it is a world where anything goes that can be negotiated. Each reality of the self gives away to reflexive questioning, irony, and ultimately the playful probing of yet another reality. The center fails to hold (Gergen, 1991: 7).

The 'postmodern condition' is something that has been widely assumed to exist by philosophers, literary theorists and social scientists alike. French philosopher Jean-Francois Lyotard's influential book, *The Postmodern Condition* (1984) described the current era as a time where 'metanarratives' such as Christianity, Marxism, and belief in scientific progress have lost their credibility. Truth, authority and reliability are all suspect and to be dispensed with. The 'real' is not to be found beyond the ways in which we describe it, and we live in 'a "perpetual present" in which the memory of tradition is gone' (Butler, 2002, loc 1687–94).

These 'tenets' of postmodernism penetrated the cultural field broadly and led to innovation in literature and art, but many social scientists also took them as guideposts in rethinking their disciplines. The relativism implied by the 'postmodern condition' was augmented by what has since been referred to as the 'linguistic turn', the roots of which lie in Swiss linguist Ferdinand de Saussure's theories. Saussure suggested that language is a formal system that has no apparent connection with the world it describes. That is, when we say 'dog', we can point to a particular four-legged animal as an example of the word, but there is nothing inherent in the dog that makes it a 'dog'. The naming is arbitrary. In Saussure's terminology, the *signifier* 'dog' has no obvious connection to the *signified* 'dog'/particular four-legged animal. The only way language makes sense is as a system of differentiation. Hence, a 'dog' makes sense because it is not a 'cat'. Stability in terminology is a social achievement, not anything determined by the world outside language itself (Macdonell, 1986: 8–12; Gergen, 1999: 24; Elder-Vass, 2012: 77–120).

Postmodernists such as Jacques Derrida went even further, suggesting that while Saussure was right in pointing out the arbitrariness of signification, his insistence that language is a formal system and that by following the rules of the system we can arrive at a conclusive interpretation of meaning, is wrong. For Derrida, *everything is text*, but 'all writing is interpretation of interpretation, with no hope of getting to an origin, closure, determinate reading, or hearing of the text or its author, who becomes irrelevant; the author vanishes' (Hollinger, 1994: 98). If postmodernists like Derrida are to be believed, Gergen's 'center' – a sense of something stable independent of 'text' – fails to hold indeed.[2]

In social psychology these ideas from linguistics and postmodern theory were incorporated into a critique of the prevailing cognitive paradigm, as discussed above. The end result is a relativist programme in which interaction and discourse take centre stage and the 'mind' practically disappears. Again, Kenneth Gergen sums the main assumptions that constructionist social psychology subscribes to:

1. The terms by which we account for the world and ourselves are not dictated by the stipulated objects of such accounts.
2. The terms and forms by which we achieve understanding of the world and ourselves are social artifacts, products of historically and culturally situated interchanges among people.

3. The degree to which a given account of the world or self is sustained across time is not dependent on the objective validity of the account but on the vicissitudes of social process.
4. Language derives its significance in human affairs from the way in which it functions within patterns of relationship.
5. To appraise existing form of discourse is to evaluate patterns of cultural life; such evaluations give voice to other cultural enclaves (see Gergen, 1994: 49–54).

Gergen's (see also Shotter, 1993; Potter, 1996) postmodern approach is openly relativist and anti-foundationalist: there is no foundation on which we can build more accurate or truer knowledge and understanding. Everything is dialogue (e.g. Gergen, 2001: 6). The (internal) mind, or the idea of (external) social structure are meaningful only when talked about by people. Hence, what *is* important is social interaction, and discourse, especially.

While this view is broadly shared by all the authors on the postmodern end of the constructionist scale, there are some subtle differences. For example, for Gergen, the focus is on *narrative*, that is, the 'storied' way in which we make sense of the world (Gergen, 1994: 185–209). He argues (as have others before him) that we need a story arc to make sense of the world, hence the importance of narrative, understood as storytelling. Shotter (1993) shares the focus on language, but for him 'life' is not rooted in texts, but conversation. Knowing is not about contemplating meaning, but about reciprocity, a response in conversation – whether a response in a current conversation, or a response to a 'conversation' understood as historical ways of talking about an issue. As we'll see below, talking about gender, for example, requires tackling not just contemporary discussions, but also historical ways of talking about women and men. Finally, Potter (1996) uses 'discourse' as an overarching concept that subsumes the idea of conversation as 'talk-in-interaction' understood as 'talk and text as parts of social practices' (1996: 105). This is perhaps the most useful concept in capturing the centrality of language in the construction of the self and the social world. As the next two chapters show, however, 'discourse' has been understood in different ways, including different ways of regarding 'reality' outside of discourse, so including a brief discussion in a section on postmodern constructionism should not be taken to cover all uses of 'discourse' in a constructionist framework. The key point about postmodern approaches to social psychology is that they share the conviction that 'whatever is, simply is [...] Once we attempt to articulate "what there is," however, we enter the world of discourse' (Gergen, 1994: 72).

Case Study: Constructing gender

Not so long ago I witnessed the birth of my first child. Without going into details, one of the anticipated – and expected – moments was when the midwife hoisted the baby up after cleaning it and announced: 'It's a baby girl!' We parents of course knew that already: the moment of revelation had come, somewhat less poetically, in one of the antenatal ultrasound scans. Whether at birth or in an ultrasound, announcing a child's sex defines, more than anything else, who we are as persons and individuals.[3] For my daughter the defining process started early: no matter how I would have liked to avoid stereotypes, her wardrobe started slowly but surely filling with 'girly' clothes even before she was born.

Pink clothes for girls and blue clothes for boys is an innocent-sounding yet indicative example of how gender difference defines social life. Girls play with dolls, boys with toy cars; girls play piano, boys play football; girls sit quiet in class, boys get detention, and so on. Although these seem like exaggerated caricatures in the Western world, it is not so long ago that girls' football was not only unknown but also practically unthinkable. For a boy raised by a single coalminer father in the 1980s England, it would have been an epic struggle to be accepted as an aspiring ballet dancer, as Stephen Daldry's film *Billy Elliott* (2000) insightfully depicts. In many of the world's cultures, the future of girls, especially, is often defined by marriage that is decided by the girl's parents – sometimes when the girls are younger than ten years old. In *all* of the world's cultures gendered expectations learned at early age follow women and men when they reach adulthood.

This is especially so in the field of labour. Among the middle classes, at least, men were considered the family 'breadwinners' whereas women took care of the home and children. Now that women have entered the waged labour force – although in very different degrees around the world and even within Europe – the differentiation between men's and women's jobs has carried over and continued, despite political interventions in the last 30 or so years. Thus, primary school teachers and nurses are still more likely to be women than men, and construction workers and engineers more likely to be men than women. And, of course, women continue to do most of domestic housework, which falls outside official labour statistics, but is a central in considering gender difference as a social issue.

The first women's rights movements of the nineteenth century, sometimes referred to as 'suffragettes' or 'first-wave feminism' fought for the right to vote (which in Europe became universal – that is, including men and women – first in Finland in 1906 and last in Switzerland in 1971) and for the right to enter universities and professions (doctors, lawyers) previously open to men only (Holmes, 2007: 110). Formal and legal equality (right to vote, non-discrimination laws) does not, however, mean social equality in a broader sense (Lorber, 2008: 538). Not only was women's work limited to particular – and almost always lower-paid – jobs, but women continued, and continue, to earn less than men in the very same jobs (see Tong, 1989: 58–61). Similarly, as mentioned above, housework has remained women's domain, although there is no reason why that should be so. Beginning in the 1960s and extending to the 1980s (Holmes, 2007: 110), 'second-wave' feminism took issue with the continuing reproduction of gender inequality, but instead of just demanding broader presentation in public life, second wave feminists switched focus to the very ways in which differences between men and women are defined and how those definitions disadvantage women as a group. This is when discussion about gender as a social construction first emerges.

Sex/gender

Differences between men and women seem obvious because of physiology: men have a penis and women have a vagina. Men and women are different. End of story.

Not quite.

If the biological difference seems common sense, it would surely be as common sense to question why on earth genitalia should dictate how well one functions as a university student, an accountant, a soldier, or a parent. Yet women and men have not been, historically speaking, equally treated in these roles, and more often than not continue to be unequally treated – almost always to the detriment of women. In other words, differences in biology also determine the 'appropriate' social roles available for women and men.

One of the earliest social scientific attempts to make sense of the impact of biology on social relationships was Anne Oakley's often-cited book *Sex, Gender and Society* (1972). She famously tried to unpack the problem of biological determinism – the idea that our social roles are determined by our biological sex – by separating sex and gender:

> 'Sex' is a biological term: 'gender' a psychological and cultural one. Common sense suggests that they are merely two ways of looking at the same division and that someone who belongs to, say, the female sex will automatically belong to the corresponding (feminine) gender. In reality this is not so. To be a man or a woman, a boy or a girl, is as much a function of dress, gesture, occupation, social network and personality, as it is of possessing a particular set of genitals (Oakley, 1972: 158).

Although similar ideas had been voiced before (Oakley, 1972: 159), Oakley's discussion was influential in the feminist movement and became a standard way of drawing attention to the social – socially constructed, if you will – aspects of gender relations and how these are institutionally reproduced in the family, in school, in the labour market, and so on. The gist of separating sex from gender was that while women and men indeed have different bodies, there is nothing 'natural' about the social roles imposed on people based on physiological differences. The argument that gender roles are defined by physical strength might make sense in prehistoric communities – and even this is much debated – but there is little universalizing relevance to the argument in the modern world. As Holmes (2007: 172) says: 'A Chinese peasant woman used to carrying heavy loads, for example, is likely to be physically stronger than a young American man who spends all day in front of the television and his computer'.[4] The attraction of the sex/gender conceptualization was in drawing attention to the way in which gender roles were discursively constructed and how the fate of an individual was not necessarily decided by her or his biological sex. Instead, the focus shifted to 'doing' gender, that is, how being a man or a woman was an active accomplishment in social interaction. The separation between sex and gender raised, however, the question of the 'naturalness' of 'sex' and led to linking the two back and also raising issues about how not only sex or gender but also sexuality influences gender roles.

Sex and gender as social constructions

Influential feminist philosopher Judith Butler has argued that gender is the most important marker of identity, because we *have* to be either male of female to be understood as 'persons' in the full sense of the word (Butler, 1990: 23). Butler and others, however, argue that biological 'sex' is not outside the sphere of discourse and hence not any more 'natural' than 'gender' is. What we understand as 'biological' is itself 'contained and constrained by beliefs about gender' (Weatherall, 2002: 81). The meanings we give to our bodies are as much socially defined as our social roles. Let me give you two examples.

First, historically speaking the idea of two separate and completely different sexes is a relatively recent one. As Thomas Laqueur painstakingly documents in his *Making Sex* (1990), until the end of the seventeenth century the philosophical and medical consensus in the West was that women and men are just aspects of one body, the male body being the standard and female bodies being considered as imperfect or incomplete versions of the male body. Sexual organs and bodily fluids were considered to have essential unity, which only manifested differently in women and men. If and when this is the case, the 'naturalness' of post-1700 ideas about two essentially different sexes needs to be looked at in a new light. Even if our science has advanced, it is the discourse about physiology that has changed, not the observable differences between women and men.

Second, the differentiation between sex and gender continues to reproduce the idea that there are two and *only two* sexes. The question that Butler and others ask is: where does this leave people born with both genitals? Or people who are born genetically female, but anatomically male? Children whose sex has been ambiguous in birth have been literally 'reconstructed' by medical professionals through surgery, because anything but an either/or case is considered a problem, despite the fact that there is no reason why these ambiguous cases should be thought of as less 'natural' than cases where the genetic, hormonal and anatomical sexes match (Holmes, 2007: 25–7). For Butler (1990), this is a sign of heteronormativity, a social order where the idea of two 'opposite' sexes that are attracted to each other is naturalized. To be something else than a woman attracted to a man and vice versa is a deviation, and 'social rules about "normal" gender and sexuality demand that you must be clear about who are boys and who are girls, so that boys and girls can grow up, fall in love with each other, and have more little boys and girls' (Holmes, 2007: 21).

The argument that sex is as much socially determined as gender touches upon some of the central issues around the 'objectivity' of the natural sciences and the practice of professions that apply the results of science (for example, medicine). While these are beyond the remit of this chapter, the contribution of feminist theory has had a wide-ranging influence on many disciplines, including (social) psychology. The study of language use is one of the subfields of psychology that illustrates the debates between a cognitive approach and a discursive, in many ways relativizing, approach.

Cognition, discourse and gender identity

One of the arenas where issues of gender essentialism and gender construction are debated is the question of language itself, or more specifically, verbal ability. This is a subset of broader debates between cognitive and discursive psychology, but also illustrates well the broader questions raised by feminist scholarship. A basic argument from cognitive psychology is that there are significant differences between (certain aspects of) female and male verbal ability: girls do better at writing tests, rate better in creative writing reviews, and suffer significantly less from defects of speech and reading such as stuttering, aphasia and dyslexia (Halpern, 2012: 119–123). Although cognitivists are quick to remind us that talking about gender differences is not about whether men are more intelligent than women, or vice versa, the differences seem to be embedded in different, gendered cognitive setups. In popular versions of the difference approach (see below) differences often become dichotomies that are putatively representative of different gender styles. For example, women's talk is characterized by 'sympathy', whereas men concentrate on 'problem-solving'; women focus on 'listening' whereas men 'lecture' (Talbot, 2010: 105). Hence, the problems in (heterosexual) relationships can be attributed to breakdowns in cross-gender communication.

Critics have pointed out that the idea that men and women 'have different languages' because of essential cognitive (and neurobiological) differences is not conclusively proved by the research literature. Although the difference paradigm seems to be in vogue – not least because of the essentializing effects of currently fashionable sociobiology – the question is far from settled. More disturbingly, as feminist psychologists have pointed out, scientific findings continue to be revised according to stereotypical beliefs about sex differences:

> Originally the left hemisphere was considered the repository of intellect and reason. The right side was the sick, bad, crazy side, the side of passion. Guess which sex was considered to have left-brain superiority? (Answer: males.) In the 1960s and 1970s however, the right brain was rediscovered. Scientists began to suspect that it was the source of genius

and inspiration, of creativity and imagination, mysticism and mathematical brilliance. Guess which sex was now thought to have 'right-brain specialization'? (Answer: males.) (Tavris, 1993: 156, quoted in Weatherall, 2002: 39.)

We can outline three possible constructionist/discursive psychology replies to the cognitive approach. First, along the more postmodern lines of Gergen, for example, we could say that science is just another narrative among others. Statistical and experimental research – often lumped under 'empiricism' in postmodern critiques – does not yield privileged knowledge, even less 'objective' knowledge, as the examples such as the left/right-brain debate above show. We can only analyse how gender differences are talked about, because we can't say anything about matters beyond discourse.[5]

A second type of constructionist argument would be to say that studying 'essential' gender differences is futile because even carefully designed and conducted research yields results that are inconclusive at best. Thus, we shouldn't think of gender as 'a stable set of traits residing within an individual psyche and reflected in behaviour', but instead as 'a discursive or ideological–symbolic concept available to construct one's self as a man or a woman' (Weatherall, 2002: 85). This does not – in my reading at least – necessarily mean that we cannot say anything about sex differences, but that we are asking the wrong questions. This is especially relevant in a culture where the difference paradigm of cognitive psychology is being popularized in self-help literature, such as John Gray's massively popular *Men are from Mars, Women are from Venus* (1992; Talbot, 2010: 110; Halpern, 2012: 6) or Deborah Tannen's *You Just Don't Understand* (1991; Talbot, 2010: 102–113), both which represent men and women as essentially different. The 'looping effects' of these kinds of books is that the difference paradigm becomes the standard way of understanding and talking about gender. That is why saying that '"men do this, women do this" is not only overgeneralized and stereotypical, it fails utterly to address the question of where "men" and "women" come from' (Cameron, 1995: 43, quoted in Talbot, 2010: 110). The social construction of gender categories should then, instead of looking for essential differences, be the focus of discursive psychology.

Finally, although the discursive approach enables us to analyse the processes of gender construction, it does not as such yet address the one question that has been at the heart of feminist inquiry from the beginning: how does gender inequality affect communication? If men and women are essentially different, no one is to blame for communication breakdowns – which, of course, is appealing to many people: the assumed essential difference 'provides a comfortable explanation for domestic disputes without pointing the finger at anybody' (Talbot, 2010: 106). The issue of *power* in social interaction is made invisible. Discourse and power is the topic of the next chapter.

Conclusion

In this chapter I have discussed a (social) psychological perspective on social constructionism, namely discursive psychology. Although discursive psychology shares with other constructionisms the idea that the human world is constituted by social interaction and language use, its specific focus is on the critique of behaviour and personality as representations of cognitive processes taking place in the brain. From this point of view, personality, for example, is not a collection of characteristics that we possess internally, but an outcome of our social interactions. 'Identity' is the term preferred to personality, because it is more fluid and changes depending on the social context. While not exclusively characteristic of discursive psychology among constructionist thought and not representative of *all* of discursive psychology, it – more than any of the other perspectives discussed in this book – draws from 'postmodern' theorizing. This means, first and foremost, abandoning any claims to privileged or 'objective' knowledge. We can only know about what we talk about, and science is just another way of talking about the world. Discursive approaches to gender have questioned the assumed essential, cognitive differences between men and women, and while 'postmodern' feminism does not represent most of feminism, it has drawn attention to the ways in which we come to know and understand what being a 'man' or 'woman' means in the first place. It also offers a liberating view: if gender is a discursive construction, changing the way we talk about gender can change ideas about what it means to be a gendered individual, and ideas about gender roles in society.

The Power of Construction: Critical Discourse Analysis

5

By now it has become more or less apparent that despite different disciplinary emphases, the social production of knowledge and beliefs through language is at the very heart of all the different perspectives on social constructionism. The ways we think about social institutions and aspects of our personal identity are shaped by interaction with other people, and the most common form of interaction is through language. 'Social intercourse' might as well, up to a point, be called 'social inter*dis*course'.

There is one aspect of social relations, however, that has so far received little attention in the perspectives on constructionism I have discussed in the preceding chapters. That is the concept of *power*. Power permeates all social relationships, and language use is imbued with power. Most of us would rather trust a doctor's diagnosis over a neighbour's in a case of suspect flu – and even more so in a case of suspect cancer. Why? The simple answer would be because the doctor's status as a trained expert and her expert language in diagnosing the symptoms make her assessments more convincing than the neighbour's. The doctor – at least in her capacity in diagnosing illness – has more power to shape how we think about the situation.

The concept of power has been an integral part of social analysis ever since Marx and Weber, and a variety of theorists have elaborated and expanded the original classical conceptualizations. My emphasis here is on what could be called the 'cultural' approach to power. From this perspective, power is seen as something that is 'diffused throughout a society rather than concentrated in sovereign organizations' (J. Scott, 2006: 128). That is to say that power is present also outside of the more obvious institutions that wield power over people, such as the state or the military. The focus, then, is on the construction of social relationships, especially domination, in everyday life. What has later been called, broadly speaking, 'critical' social theory (Calhoun, 1995; Agger, 2006)[1] is especially interested in the role of power in the shaping of the social world. I have chosen *critical discourse analysis* (CDA) and especially the work of Norman Fairclough, its best-known proponent, to represent the fourth distinctive perspective on social constructionism (e.g. Fairclough, 1989; 1992; 1995a, b; 2003).

Although I am tempted, I will refrain from using the term 'critical construc-tionism'[2] and retain Fairclough's own term, because there are some good grounds for questioning whether critical discourse analysis should be included in a listing of different strands of constructionism at all. Especially in his later writings (Fairclough, Jessop and Sayer, 2002; Fairclough, 2003: 14), Fairclough has identified himself explicitly with critical realism, a view that is often pitted against constructionism (Bhaskar, 1993; Shotter, 1993; Elder-Vass, 2012). However, at the same time he readily acknowledges that reality is socially constructed, but the construction process is constrained by the context in which the discourse takes place (Fairclough, 2003: 8). In his most construc-tionist line of thought, Fairclough states:

> Social practice does not merely 'reflect' a reality which is independent of it; social practice is in an active relationship to reality, and it changes reality. The world that human beings live in is a massively humanly cre-ated world, a world created in social practice. [...] As far as the social world is concerned, social structures not only determine social practice, they are also a product of social practice. And more particularly, social structures not only determine discourse, they are also a product of dis-course (Fairclough, 1989:, 37–8).

As can be seen, Fairclough's perspective resembles the basic propositions of constructionist thought made earlier by Berger and Luckmann, for example (see Fairclough, 1992: chapters 5 and 6). Therefore, although Fairclough might nowadays shun the label 'social constructionist',[3] critical discourse analysis can be validly included as an example of a fourth kind of construc-tionism. It has affinities with the other kinds of constructionist thought described above, discursive psychology especially, but also has unique charac-teristics which separate it from the others.

Like all theorizations of discourse, critical discourse analysis has been much influenced by the work of Michel Foucault, the French scholar who con-tributed to many fields of academic inquiry, including philosophy, sociology and history. Foucault emphasized the constitutive (constructive) nature of dis-course (Foucault, 1995: 31–9; see Fairclough, 1992: 39–48) and, especially in his later works, the political nature of discourse. In Fairclough's (1992: 49–50) words, 'the view of the nature of power in modern societies which Foucault develops [...] places discourse and language at the heart of social practices and processes'. Discourse is the building material of the human world, but at the same time intrinsically interwoven with questions of power. Although CDA often shares interest in Foucault with discursive psychology, CDA emphasizes the role of power more than any perspective and, as I will show below, has taken the discussion beyond Foucault.

There are two main points that set CDA apart from the other perspectives discussed in this book. First, whereas the other approaches have grown out of the social sciences and ended up emphasizing the role of language in social analysis, in CDA the process is more or less reverse. Fairclough (1992: 12–36, 1995a: 20–34), an emeritus Professor of Language in Social Life, is mainly concerned with expanding earlier linguistic theories to include more social elements. That is why some of the discussions in Fairclough's work may seem a bit baffling to the beginning sociologist and also why I will mostly concentrate on the implications of his discourse theory to the wider understanding of processes of social construction. However, the two shouldn't be seen as separate. One of attractions of CDA is that it offers a solid theoretical base combined with a detailed method for analysing social life.

Second, and more central to our concerns here, is CDA's focus on *hegemony* and *ideology* as central concepts in analysing discourse. Power was the focus of much of Foucault's work, but as Fairclough (1992: 59) puts it, Foucault's 'neglect of struggle' and his avoidance of the concept of ideology can make the analysis one-sided, concentrating on 'the perspective of the powerful, of those whose problem is preserving social order and sustaining domination'. CDA combines a broadly Marxist approach to social struggle with the analysis of discourse, making it possible to analyse both domination *and* emancipation and social transformation.

The above said has two important implications for our current endeavour. First, I will need to flesh out the concepts of hegemony and ideology and discuss what kind of constructionism emerges from the application of these concepts. Second, more explicitly than any of the other perspectives, and in direct opposition to some of the more 'postmodern' strands of social psychology, analysing the relationship between discourse and the 'real world' is central to CDA. Defining characteristics of CDA are its insistence on the existence of social structure outside of discourse and a focus on the study of the reciprocal relation between language use and non-linguistic structures. CDA is an original approach to analysing the often-problematic relation between the two, which I will discuss in the latter part of the chapter, before moving on to an excursion on how to use CDA in practical analysis of media discourse.

Power and hegemony

Social power can be defined as 'an agent's intentional use of causal powers to affect the conduct of other participants in the social relations that connect them together' (Scott, 2001: 1). In its simple form this means that, for example, as residents of particular country we have an obligation to pay taxes on the money we earn in that country. In this case the state uses power in order to get a share of our income. State power is manipulative and coercive, because we will be punished in the form of fines if we don't pay our taxes on time, or we might even be imprisoned for not paying our debt to the state. For Max Weber, who thought that power was 'one of the most important elements of social action' (Weber, 1978: 941), and for the 'mainstream approach' (Scott, 2001: 6) that developed Weber's ideas further, the study of power concentrates on recognizable institutions, such as the state, and decision-making in those institutions.

Another approach to social power, developed in the writings of Antonio Gramsci and made popular especially by Foucault, sees power as more pervasive of social relations and in a less 'obvious' sense. From this perspective, power is not only an attribute of organizations and institutions that explicitly exercise it, but permeates all social relationships. It is also not primarily coercive, but rather persuasive, in nature. Socialization and the internalization of shared values and habits create *self-discipline*, a central concept in Foucault's work (Foucault, 1978; 1995). Remember the example used by Berger and Luckmann about spilling soup? The child is reminded of not spilling the soup up to a point when she internalizes the norm and stops spilling it. Power is constantly at work in this process, although after a point it becomes 'invisible'. We conform to expectations – in differing degrees – even without anyone constantly reminding us about the proper ways to act and be.

We rarely give any thought to most of the things – such as not spilling soup – we do in everyday life. These ways of doing things have become common sense to us. As Berger and Luckmann argued, without a commonsensical attitude, everyday life would be impossible. Consider what your day would be like if you stopped to think about why or on what grounds do we have to wear clothes to work, wait until the traffic lights are green, pay at the counter of the coffee shop and so on. Problematizing every action would mean you would hardly be out of the door before it was time to go to bed again! (Besides, why do we sleep at night, not during the day?)

Although common sense is obviously something we need to get by everyday life, it is not as 'innocent' as it may seem. Unlike some of the other perspectives on social constructionism, which also highlight the importance of the concept of common sense, CDA argues that 'common sense [...] is itself an *effect of power*' (Fairclough, 1989: 92; emphasis in the original). Our commonsensical conceptions of proper practices are outcomes of a process of selection where alternative ways of doing and thinking are discarded. In other words, common sense conceptions are results of a power struggle. For example, there is nothing inherent in eating soup that precludes spilling. We might eat soup by pouring it on our foreheads and trying to catch whatever we can with our tongues. However, even the suggestion sounds absurd, because eating soup the way we do has become a *naturalized* way of thinking. We really do not see an alternative, where there could be one, at least in principle. Put in more elegant terms, naturalization is the 'recognition of legitimacy through misrecognition of arbitrariness' (Bourdieu, 1994).

When a single practice or a way of thinking becomes the *only* legitimate one, supplanting other interpretations, it has become hegemonic. *Hegemony* is a term coined by the influential Italian Marxist thinker Antonio Gramsci (1971). Gramsci differentiated 'domination' – that is, state power in the narrow coercive sense – from 'intellectual and moral leadership' which inspires certain types of action, and which he called 'hegemony' (Fairclough, 1995: 93,

Larrain, 2006: 86). In contrast to coercive power, hegemonic consensus is achieved by persuasion. As Fairclough (1992: 92) puts it: 'Hegemony is about constructing alliances, and integrating rather than simply dominating subordinate classes, through concessions [...] to win their consent.' More recent elaborations of Gramsci's ideas (for example, Thompson, 1990; Fairclough, 1992) have noted, however, that although the concept of hegemony usefully differentiates between coercive and persuasive power, both should be considered aspects of domination. A hegemonic situation is achieved only through the use of power, whatever the type of power might be. Critical discourse analysis expands this view by focusing on the central role of discourse in achieving hegemony.

Discourse and ideology

Now that we've discussed the notions of power and hegemony, a question still remains: How does a practice or a way of thinking achieve a hegemonic position? One example would be the criminalization of practices, a process that often not only denotes which practices are not permissible, but also which practices are recommendable. Power in modern societies is, however, not only about coercion such as criminalization. Rather, and following Foucault's ideas discussed above, power is increasingly exercised through the use of persuasive language. When 'proper' ways of thinking about and doing things are constructed from a particular perspective, giving a one-sided account that ignores the variety of practices, discourse is said to function *ideologically* (Chouliaraki and Fairclough, 1999: 26). For example, when the characteristics of a group of people are represented as derivable from their ethnic or religious background (e.g. 'Muslim terrorists'), the discourse 'irons out' the variety of beliefs, practices and ways of thinking in the group. Hegemony is the peak of ideology, the point when all alternative constructions are suppressed in favour of one dominating view.

The concept of ideology has a history dating back to the very beginnings of social science, although it has also been used as frequently, if not more, in political talk (for excellent overviews, see Thompson, 1984; 1990). For our purposes it is important to differentiate between the everyday use of ideology and the *critical conception of ideology* (Thompson, 1990: 7). In everyday talk, ideology often denotes a worldview or a (secular) belief system. Thus, we hear about communist ideology, nationalism, neoliberalism, and ecological ideology, for example (see, for example, Macridis, 1992). While this way of using 'ideology' is rooted in the history of the concept, critical discourse analysis uses it in a different sense.

For CDA (and the critical tradition of social science that it draws upon), ideology is intimately tied with the question of power in discourse. Concisely defined, the critical tradition sees ideology as 'meaning in the service of power' (Thompson, 1990: 8). Speaking in the plural, Fairclough defines ideologies as:

[C]onstructions of reality (the physical world, social relations, social identities), which are built into various dimensions of the forms/meanings of discursive practices, and which contribute to the production, reproduction or transformation of relations of domination (Fairclough, 1992: 87; see Thompson, 1990: 56).

The classic example of this is the representation of guerrilla fighters in the news. The choice of words for their presentation is crucial here: are they 'terrorists' or 'freedom fighters?' Whatever the choice, discourse can be said to work ideologically when a description paints a one-sided picture of an event or a person, at the same time shutting out alternative interpretations.

With this conception of ideology in mind, we can turn back to the previous discussion on power and hegemony. What I referred to as 'common sense' above is 'substantially, though not entirely, *ideological*' (Fairclough, 1989: 84; emphasis in the original). Because common sense naturalizes our conceptions of everyday life, it is the most effective way of sustaining hegemony, that is, an exclusive interpretation of reality. When common sense works this way, it becomes *'common sense in the service of sustaining unequal relations of power'* (Fairclough, 1989: 84; emphasis in the original). Returning to the question posed above: How does a practice or a way of thinking achieve a hegemonic position? The answer can be summarized as: ideological discourse acts as a vehicle for achieving hegemony.

Unlike the use of coercive and explicit power, the ideological function of discourse is often hidden. As Fairclough (1989: 85) notes:

> Ideology is most effective when its workings are least visible. If one becomes aware that a particular aspect of common sense is sustaining power inequalities at one's own expense, it ceases to *be* common sense, and may cease to have capacity to sustain power inequalities, i.e. to function ideologically. And invisibility is achieved when ideologies are brought to discourse not as explicit elements of the text, but as the background assumptions which on the one hand lead the text producer to 'textualize' the world in a particular way and on the other hand lead the interpreter to interpret the text in a particular way. (Emphasis in the original.)

It feels obvious that, for example, it is in any ruling government's interest to produce discourse that presents its actions in a favourable light. But because of political divisions, the people on the receiving end of political discourse will always be either positively or negatively predisposed towards these messages. It is indeed a rare thing for overtly political discourse to be unanimously accepted and considered as 'common sense'. Therefore, in order to function as effectively as possible, ideological discourse must work more subtly.

This means that one of the tasks of CDA is what could be called 'unmasking'. Unmasking examines 'the effect of ideologies in "ironing out" (i.e. suppressing) aspects of practices [...] links ideologies to "mystification" and "mis-recognition"' (Chouliaraki and Fairclough, 1999: 26). Therefore, unmasking means studying not only what is said, but also what is *not* said. 'Silences' in discourse are very effective in buffering ideology by simplifying representations of social reality.

In short summary, power functions through discourse, and when discourse works to sustain unequal power relations it is ideological discourse. There are, however, four further points on discourse and ideology that I would like to add. First, the above examples of ideological uses of discourse are not meant to implicate that the state, the news media, or our best friends are deliberately seeking to corrupt our minds by using ideological discourse in everyday interaction. Although ideology is often closely related to particular social institutions, it does not mean that ideological use of language is always conscious. On the contrary, as discussed above, it is exactly the 'common sense' assumptions we bring into our discourse that most effectively reproduce our conceptions of social relationships and our social identity.

Second, unlike some earlier Marxist theories of ideology (see Thompson, 1990: 85–97; Fairclough, 1992: 29) that focus on the reproduction of the class interests of the powerful, CDA emphasizes that ideology can be both a vehicle for reproduction (status quo) *and* transformation (change) (Fairclough, 1992: 89). The fact that ideological discourse is restricted by the social context of language use does not – and cannot – tell the analyst the actual ideological effects of discourse. Ideology can be resisted and made into a vehicle for transformation through alternative interpretations. Therefore the concept of *struggle* is central to a dialectical view of ideology, such as CDA endorses.

Third, one of the criticisms levelled against CDA is that it concentrates narrowly on the reproduction and transformation of *class* relations. While CDA explicitly draws from Marxist social theory, and although Fairclough himself in his early work talks almost exclusively about social class, the study of ideological discourse in modern societies extends and should extend to *all* kinds of unequal relations of power. Therefore, critical discourse analysis can be used to study the reproduction of gender relations in media discourse, for example. Or, we could examine the changing understanding of ethnicity in the public sphere. Gender, age, ethnicity and race, for example, are difference markers that are equally important to class in studying ideological uses of power in modern societies. John B. Thompson argues that 'it would be quite misleading, in my view, to maintain that class relations are the *only*, or in all circumstances the *primary*, structural feature of social contexts with reference to which the analysis of ideology should be carried out' (Thompson, 1990; 94–5; emphases in the original. See Chouliaraki and Fairclough, 1999: 24).

Finally, although CDA is explicitly 'textually oriented', the critical perspective extends the study of ideological struggle beyond text, the point being that ideological struggle happens not only *in* language, but *over* language. Or, put differently, discourse is both the site of power struggles and the stake in power struggles (Fairclough, 1989: 74). In addition to academic analysis of texts,

CDA also advocates 'critical language awareness' (Fairclough, 1989: 234–47; 1995b: 219–52). Critical language awareness focuses on the role of language use in social institutions, particularly in the area of education. Fairclough (1995b: 233–52), for example, has discussed the 'appropriate' use of English language in schools and how language is often represented as 'if it were a part of the natural environment over which [the pupils] have no control' (Fairclough, 1989: 239). This obviously is contrary to the critical (constructionist) view that sees language as socially constituted and constituting. Representing language in such one-sided light is ideological in the very sense outlined above and the task of critical language awareness is to draw attention to the ideological understandings of language, especially in education, but also in other areas of social life (see Fairclough, 1989: 234–6).

Analysing discourse and society critically

Social science, and sociology in particular, owes a great deal to Marx for introducing 'dialectical logic' (Chouliaraki and Fairclough, 1999: 32) into the study of human interaction. While Marx himself concentrated on the economic side of social life, and can be argued to have overemphasized the role of social structure in his own work, his ideas have been since modified and taken further by many social theorists. In CDA, thinking dialectically means that discourse has a dual nature: it constructs the world, but also draws from it.

The dialectical view of discourse and society has grown out of two opposing critiques of ideas that CDA employs. First, CDA is critical of structurally oriented Marxism that sees social structure as the primary defining characteristic of social life. From a dialectical perspective, taking this view into its logical conclusion leaves little room for individual action. Therefore, CDA posits that individuals construct the social world through discourse and that these discursive constructions have very 'real' effects, such as when government policies (that are words and texts) affect the price of housing, for example. The second critique is directed against the more 'postmodern' versions of social constructionism that espouse the productive force of discourse, but also see it as singularly constitutive of society, ignoring any structural forces beyond discourse. While the construction of the human world is considered a discursive process in CDA, according to Fairclough 'these [discursive] practices are constrained by the fact that they inevitably take place within a constituted, material reality, with preconstituted "objects" and preconstituted social subjects' (Fairclough, 1992: 60). CDA divides its attention between both discourse *and* the institutional framework where discourse is used. Fairclough (1992; 1995) has illustrated the relation between discourse and social structure by dividing the analysis into three levels: text, discourse practice and social practice.

The level of text is the bread and butter of CDA. Especially the more linguistically oriented approaches to CDA focus on this level, although never exclusively. Fairclough further divides the analysis of texts into three levels: the constructions of knowledge and beliefs, the constructions of interpersonal relations between actors, and the identities of actors constructed in discourse. Thus, a news story, for example, always constructs an event from a particular point of view, being one representation out of many. Similarly, news constructs identities for the actors involved in the event, and those identities are in interaction, creating subject positions for the actors.

For example, when a news story about a demonstration says that 'a riot was suppressed by the police' and has a police official as an expert 'witness', the story is one-sided. Already the word choice of 'riot' constructs the demonstrators as the 'bad people' in the narrative, and because the police official is given the voice of the expert, the story creates a sense that the official point of view is the right one and police action (the vague 'suppressed' hiding a sense of active participation – using violence, for example) is justified. The representation of the event, the identities of the actors and their interpersonal relations all support the same construction. This is clearly a case of a text that has an ideological bias, which is the particular focus of CDA.

Now, it would be tempting to conclude from the text that the news media is controlled by the state and that it feeds one-sided information to the public. There are, however, two caveats to be made. First, without knowledge of the production process of the media, only tentative conclusions can be drawn about the motivations of the news industry. Second, texts alone do not dictate how people read them and the interpretations that they make. In Fairclough's terminology discourse practice denotes the production and consumption processes of texts that further shape our understanding of the topic in question. Discourse practice is the mediating level between text and sociocultural practice (the level of social structure). Full understanding of the discourse practices pertaining to a particular media event would ideally include an ethnographic study of the production and consumption of the event; how editorial processes on the one hand, and reading, listening and TV watching processes on the other shape the image of the world as represented in the news. However, the text itself can give the analyst clues to the production and consumption processes. By looking at the intertextual properties of texts, CDA analyses ways in which other texts are used in the presentation of news. Most news providers work within the logic of consumer capitalism, which means that they have to sell their product. In order to do so, the discourse found on the pages of the newspaper, for example, has to conform to certain expectations. Therefore the production of news is based (often implicitly) on a sense of what the public wants to hear. This is not to say that news is made with only the consumer in mind, without any reference to something that could be called 'the truth'. But it means that the truth is packaged in forms easily recognizable by the public. This is where intertextuality comes into play. Another, more blatant example would be the marketing of popular culture media, such as books and music. How many times have you seen a new book advertised as the 'New Harry Potter,' or an album by a new artist as the 'New Beatles', 'New Madonna', 'New Snoop Dogg', or whatever? Intertextuality 'works' because consumers of texts make intertextual connections with topics they are already familiar with, even if they do know little or nothing about the content of the particular text.

Finally, the level of sociocultural practice refers to the broad social and cultural contexts where discursive communication happens. The analysis of sociocultural practice can refer to different levels: the immediate institutional context where the discourse is embedded in, a national framework, or even a global context (Fairclough, 1995a: 62). Unlike approaches (inspired by postmodernism) that claim that 'context' should be considered as ever moving and part of the process of construction (e.g. Silverman, 2007: 105), CDA insists that we can explain features of discourse by referring to the broader social and cultural practices of language use. What aspects of the broader context are included can vary, but Fairclough (1995a: 62) helpfully differentiates between economic, political (concerned with issues of power and ideology) and cultural (concerned with questions of value and identity) aspects. I will discuss these in the next section.

Case study: News media discourse and power

> Some time ago, I had an intriguing conversation with a five-year-old about elephants. 'Have you ever seen an elephant?' I asked. 'Sure,' he replied, 'there was a show on TV.' 'No,' I said, 'I mean a real elephant. We could go to the zoo.' 'No, that's okay,' he said. 'I already saw it.' He saw no difference between an actual elephant and a flickering image on a screen. (Finch, 2007: 86)

The above example, from a guide to writing about and through the senses in fiction, is indicative of the wide-ranging effects of living in a media-saturated world. While it would be exaggerating to say (again, à la postmodernists such as Jean Baudrillard) that images on TV, in this case, have become reality itself for people like the above five-year old, it is clear that much of the what we know about the world nowadays is mediated knowledge. In this section I want to look at the news media, in particular; how they construct our sense of the world, and our sense of our selves. I will begin by discussing the broad changes that the proliferation of media technologies has entailed. I will then look at newspaper headlines as example of how knowledge, social relationships and identities are constructed, and discuss how to analyse the ideological functions of these constructions. Finally, I will situate the news media in the broader contexts of production, reception and sociocultural practice.

The mediazation of modern culture

The industrial revolution and the social changes it entailed were the main focus of the classics of social science. Urbanization, the emergence of an unskilled working class, secularization and other developments attracted, and continue to attract, the attention of social scientists. With the exception of media studies – a comparably late addition to the field of social science – surprisingly little attention has been paid to another, more recent and worldwide development: the communication revolution. Where the face-to-face situation was the paramount mode of social interaction only a hundred years ago (and still considered such by Berger and Luckmann, for example), it is safe to say that in the developed world mediated interaction has now become the primary mode of interaction.

Although the emergence of social media such as Facebook, Twitter and others has made it difficult to keep up with the empirical changes in the field, John B. Thompson's (1990; 1995) theoretical insights are still a useful guide to understanding how the media change social life. Thompson (1995: 34–6) outlines four major aspects: First, the development of communication media provide 'mediated historicity', that is, a sense of the past that is dependent on 'an ever expanding reservoir of mediated symbolic forms' (Thompson, 1995: 34). Unlike in oral cultures, where the limits of memory can be said to have been the limits of history (but not myth), our knowledge of the past is now 'inscribed' in books, newspapers, films and so on. Second, whereas in previous times 'the world' that people lived in was constructed out of personal experience – mostly from local community, sometimes through physical travel – the world is open to us through mediated forms. This 'mediated worldliness' is an important part of the everyday experience of what is commonly called globalization. When we travel to distant lands, for example, we are a bit like the boy who saw the elephant on TV – we almost always have an image of the destination long before reaching it. Third, our sense of belonging is increasingly what Thompson (1995: 35) calls 'mediated sociality'. Written in the first half of the 1990s, Thompson's analysis was apt and prescient of the ways in which the groups and communities we belong to are increasingly constructed online, in the social media. Finally, with 'space–time compression' the transmitting of news, for example, has ceased to be dependent on the speed of physical transportation (which of course has increased many-fold at the same time). Now global communication is – theoretically at least – possible at a push of a 'send' button.

Thompson calls these developments the *mediazation* of culture (Thompson, 1990: 12–20; 1995: 46). They are embedded in the structural development of media organizations, which have expanded massively since the first commercial book publishers of the fifteenth century started their business. The effects, however, range far beyond the emergence of a new section of the economy. Most importantly, for Thompson, the expansion of the media has created a new form of social interaction, which he refers to as 'mediated quasi-interaction' (Thompson, 1995: 84–7). This is communication which is directed to an unspecified audience, as opposed to specific recipients in face-to-face interaction and mediated interaction like letters or phone calls. Books, films, postings on Twitter and so on are produced for a potentially infinite number of recipients. Mediated quasi-interaction is also characterized by one-way communication, where the production of symbolic forms is removed from their audiences and where audiences have little or no chance of responding. The development of social media and online interaction has changed this somewhat since the 1990s, but it is fair to question whether this really amounts to radical change. It is true that responses to a news story are more immediate online, when compared to old style letters to the editor, for example, but issues of access and moderation continue to be important factors in considering the nature of communication. We are increasingly engaged in 'online sociality', but the form of sociality is different – and not necessarily at the expense of face to face interaction, as the wilder versions of 'virtual reality' would like us to believe (Thompson, 1995: 87).

'Mediazation' catches many of the changes mediated (and quasi-mediated) modernity entails for social interaction. Against more utopian visions, mediazation does *not* mean that the human world becomes an entirely virtual construction. There are significant global differences between access to the internet, for example. Similarly, mediazation is not just simply a technical process which expands our sense of the human world. It has also potentially deeply ideological implications, as the following analysis of war reporting demonstrates.

Ideology and journalism

Critical discourse analysis is unique among the constructionist perspectives discussed in this book when it comes to attention to linguistic detail. Although always rooted in the sociocultural context, CDA aims to show how linguistic detail can influence our interpretations of events reported in the news. The range of linguistic aspects that a CDA 'toolkit' can include is wide, so much so that like with any type of discourse analysis, only rarely can a practical analysis pay attention to *all* aspects of texts (for an example of the full apparatus, see Fairclough, 1992: 225–40; Richardson, 2007: 46–74). Hence my brief example here will be similarly limited.

I will use Richardson's (2007: 178–219) insightful analysis of the British newspaper reporting of the 2003 invasion of Iraq by the United States and the United Kingdom, Australia and Poland. War reporting is a specific genre, of course, not least because so much of the information about the events in the field comes filtered through official channels (press releases, limited reporter access and so on). At the same time, war reporting is a good example of how action is discursively justified by constructing a clear sense of 'us' and 'them'. It is these transitive aspects of war reporting that I will concentrate on here. According to Mills, 'the study of transitivity is concerned with how actions are represented; what kind of actions appear in a text, who does them and to whom they are done' (Mills, 1995: 143–4, quoted in Richardson, 2007: 54). Transitivity, in other words, is concerned with the imputation of agency and, subsequently, responsibility. As we will see, the choice of transitive aspects in news texts can have significant ideological effects.

Following Richardson, I will use newspaper headlines as examples of ideological reporting. Although headlines don't exhaust a news story, they play an important role in drawing the readers' attention to a topic and orienting them to what is being said. Van Dijk (1988: 53) argues that headlines function as summaries of news stories. Richardson (2007: 199–200), however, argues that headline construction in tabloids, especially, does not necessarily follow a logic of summary. Instead, they seem to conform to Dor's (2003: 697) contention that 'tabloid headlines rarely summarize their stories' and 'in many cases are not even informative'. Instead, the reader is presented with a 'fairly complex riddle' that is then solved in the text itself. The ideologically interesting aspect is, nevertheless, that the headline orients the reader to the rest of the story and choice of how to represent transitive processes is key to understanding this. I will not go into the generic differences between tabloid and broadsheet papers, except to note that nominalization – the representation of processes as states of being (see below), which masks agency – seems to be much more common in tabloids (Richardson, 2007: 203–4).

At the beginning of the invasion, *The Daily Telegraph* (a national broadsheet) reported: 'Allies launch their onslaught on tyranny from air, land and sea' (21 March 2003). The headline not only tells the reader what has happened, but provides a justification as well. Instead of 'their onslaught on Iraq' – not to mention 'their invasion' – the allies 'onslaught on tyranny' justifies the use of force in a situation where opinions about the invasion were far from harmonious in Britain. In the beginning of the invasion, headlines such as the above would still talk about the armed forces as 'them', but when the operations dragged on and their casualties became more apparent, the war effort was identified with 'us', especially in tabloid headlines:

'Barely 18, our youngest soldier in the conflict' (*Daily Mail*, 1 April 2003)
'Crusade for all our war heroes' (*Daily Express*, 15 April 2003)
'Hero Brits mourned' (*Sun*, 18 April 2003)
'Free our men' (*Daily Mirror*, 29 April 2003)

The masking of agency plays an important role in the ideological construction of 'us' and 'them'. This is perhaps most apparent in the reporting of the negative consequences of 'our' actions, as in the following headlines:

'Missiles hit Red Crescent maternity hospital' (*Independent*, 3 April 2003)
'Maternity Unit bomb kills three' (*Daily Mirror*, 3 April 2003)
'Rocket kills teenager in Iran' (*Financial Times*, 9 April 2003)

In all of the cases, US forces launched the bombs and rockets, but the reader would be unaware of this without reading the actual story. There is no agent in these headlines, no one doing the bombing. The ideological significance of this is apparent if we change the headline into 'US bombs maternity unit and kills three' (Richardson, 2007: 202).

Nominalization (processes represented as states of being) masks agency in headlines like the *Sun*'s (21 March 2003) 'Baghdad burning': this tells us what is going on, not what exactly has happened or why. As Richardson (2007: 206) comments: 'While it is inconceivable that any reader of the newspaper would be unaware that Baghdad was burning because the US had bombed it, nevertheless, the headline acts to background this politically uncomfortable fact: US bombs were burning Baghdad, razing its civilian infrastructure, its schools and its homes.' Similarly, the *Daily Mirror*'s (26 March 2003) headline 'A volatile region is in chaos' tells us the state of things, but nothing about how that came to be. Again, replacing the statement that the region 'is in chaos' with a description of the process – 'US brings chaos to Middle East' (Richardson, 2007: 206) – shows that the linguistic choices in newspaper headlines are also ideological choices.

The above is necessarily a snapshot of complex 'textually-oriented discourse analysis' (Fairclough, 1992: 37): There are many more examples of ideological headlines discourse and many other linguistic aspects in addition to transitivity in Richardson's analysis. But the examples show that if (and when) we conceive of ideology as 'meaning in the service of power', as representations of the world that by virtue of their one-sidedness serve the interests of certain actors – in this case the governments responsible for the war – subtle textual choices, especially when repeated in hegemonic discourse, can have significant effects on how the world is perceived. Textual analysis can never by itself tell us how the texts are received and interpreted, but combined with broader analysis of the contexts of interpretation, they offer a powerful way of thinking about how the world beyond our first-hand experience is constructed.

News media in the global and local contexts of capitalism

As we found in the beginning of this section, mediazation is a ubiquitous aspect of the modern world. But mediazation has happened alongside another now-ubiquitous development: the emergence of global capitalism. After 'history ended', that is, following the abolition of the socialist regimes in the Soviet Union and its European satellites, there has been no challenge to the globalization of the capitalist mode of production. The People's Republic of China is officially communist, yes, but also one of the most significant providers of cheap labour, raw materials and financial services for the global market. With the exception of North Korea, the world is fully integrated into a capitalist system. Although perhaps not immediately apparent, this situation has important implications for a critical analysis of the media in the modern world. When searching for answers to the questions about *why* the media works ideologically – in Fairclough's terms, looking at explanation on the level of sociocultural practice (1989: 140–141) – the answer is to be found in the framework of unchallenged global capitalism.

One of the lasting legacies of the Marxist tradition is the idea that material conditions determine cultural forms. There are myriad variations of this idea, and in this context we can gloss over questions about what Marx and Engels meant by 'determine'. But as Wayne (2003: 135) – speaking specifically of the media – says, Marxism assumes that 'the dominant social and economic relations will be manifested in the politics of the cultural values that the media produce so that the media will in general further the reproduction of the relations of production'. Is this a reasonable proposition? Wayne (2003: 136) argues that it is (see also Molyneux, 2012):

> If it were *not* a reasonable proposition and starting point then one would expect to see the mainstream news media calling capitalism into question on a regular basis; one would expect to find them attacking the profit motive routinely, pointing out the irrationality of capitalism's priorities, highlighting its wastefulness, attacking *wealthy* minorities that control vast resources rather than the poor and the vulnerable (such as asylum seekers), and linking the various tragedies, discontents and crises which they find in the world back to the capitalist relations of production. (Emphases in the original.)

It is arguable whether textually oriented critical discourse analysis has always been faithful to the Marxist premise that links texts to their material contexts (Richardson, 2007: 28; see below). Even if we want to avoid the more determinist versions of Marxism, it is reasonable to argue that although the mainstream news media sometimes lend voice to views critical of capitalism, or voice such views themselves, the system itself is rarely questioned. In other terms, the mainstream media can be alternative, but almost never oppositional (Wayne, 2003: 135). As Richardson (2007: 135–6) puts it: 'There is little that divides the British public along class lines as straightforwardly as newspaper readership. [...] That said, very little journalism actually *discusses* capitalism – in other words, what it is, how it works, the arguments for and against its perpetuation and so on' (emphasis in the original). In other words, capitalism is naturalized as the framework for news production.

The effects of capitalism are observable on the more local and less abstract level as well. In many countries, as Richardson notes about Britain above, class lines divide the news audiences. For example, of the manual working classes that make up about 50 per cent of the population, 5 percent read *The Times* (a conservative broadsheet), but 41 per cent read *The Sun* (a tabloid). In the managerial/upper professional class the numbers are reversed: 55 per cent read *The Times*, against only a 6 per cent readership for *The Sun* (Richardson, 2007: 81). This means that much of the advertisement revenue is directed towards the upper end of the broadsheet market, where the buying power is. Mercedes Benz and BMW have full page advertisements in the *Financial Times*, but you would be hard pressed to find them in the *Daily Mirror*. The effect of this is that the advertisement revenue enables broadsheets to concentrate on 'serious' news, whereas tabloids rely on mass sales by concentrating mainly on 'drama, surprise, personalities, sex, scandal and crime'

(Richardson, 2007: 91). If we think of news as important sources for constructing a view of the world, it makes a big difference whether your daily dose
of information about the world beyond your immediate experience is about
the latest changes is European Union legislation or the latest changes in the fat
percentage of your favourite celebrity. The suggestion is *not* that one topic is
inherently more important than the other, but rather that the class context of
news audiences creates certain kinds of news, which in turn reproduce class
positions and tastes – a topic central to the critical analysis of discursive and
social change.

Conclusion

In this chapter I have discussed Critical discourse analysis (CDA) as a form of
constructionism. Drawing from a mix of linguistic and critical (Marxist) social
theory, CDA is unique among constructionisms in its focus on power and ideology. Ideology is conceived in the critical sense of the term, as meaning in the
service of power. The aim of CDA is to map how linguistic choices construct
the world from a particular perspective – at the same time suppressing other
perspectives – and how knowledge, social relations and identities are reproduced and transformed in ideological discourse. When a particular view of
representing the world has no challengers, the discourse has become hegemonic. Unlike more traditional Marxist theories, which emphasize the role of
reproduction, CDA sees hegemony as a dialectical process that is achieved
through struggle, hence enabling reproduction *and* transformation of social
reality. Although CDA often emphasizes textual analysis and the study of the
ideological effects of discourse, a rounded *critical* analysis of texts also consid-
ers the contexts of text production and consumption. This contextual analysis
plays a central role on moving beyond the micro level of communicative events
to broader explanations of the effects of discourse. The global and local contexts of news texts and their production and consumption demonstrate how
CDA works in practice.

Constructionisms and Critiques

6

My first personal experience of sociological pigeonholing happened at an international conference in the early 2000s. At the conference dinner after party a colleague introduced me to a table of delegates: 'This is Titus, he's a social constructionist, but he's an OK guy.' The key word here is 'but': I was an OK guy *despite* the fact that I was a 'constructionist'. I sat down with some trepidation, but it turned out to be a peaceful evening. The comment nevertheless demonstrated to me that constructionism was a dividing line in the academy, not just in highbrow theoretical debates, but in everyday practice.

Constructionism has indeed had its critics from very early on. Chronologically these can be grouped into several 'waves': First, in American sociology, the emergence of symbolic interactionism as a distinct field of sociology (and social psychology) generated heated debate from the late 1950s onwards (Reynolds, 1993). Second, the reaction to postmodernist ideas in social science – especially in the wake of the notorious Sokal hoax, where American physicist Alan Sokal got a paper published in influential cultural studies journal *Social Text* and then confessed that the text was basically gobbledygook attempting to emulate postmodern conventions – sparked a discussion that was to characterize most of the social scientific divisions in the 1980s and 1990s. Most recently, the rise of 'critical realism' has prompted some comments which dismiss constructionism as an antiquated and untenable approach, but also discussions where the potential positive contribution of (different types of) constructionism is evaluated in light of realist meta-theorizing (especially Elder-Vass, 2012).

These critiques have come from both inside and outside the constructionist tradition. The purpose of the internal critics has often been – without much success – to define what a 'properly' constructionist social science should look like. The simple fact that no agreement exists even among those who consider themselves 'constructionists' is a sign both of the diversity of the field and of a reluctance to characterize constructionism as a singular 'theory'. The external critics, in turn, have focused on the deficiencies and biases of constructionism, especially its inability to answer certain questions. Not a small amount of this critique has arisen as a response to sometimes not-so-gentle critiques of 'traditional' social science from the constructionist camp itself. As shown in the above chapters, all of the different constructionist perspectives discussed here emerged more or less as critiques of currently hegemonic traditions in their respective fields.

Before I move on to the particular topics of contention, it is worth repeating one thing here: if the point of this book – that, at the end of the day, we should talk about constructionisms in the plural instead of a single entity – is taken seriously (as I think it should be), then the obvious first line of defence against critics is to point out how a particular critique does not apply to *all* types of constructionism. Indeed, as Rom Harré (1998: xi) puts it: 'Catch-all terms like "realism", "constructionism" and so on, invite endless and distracting debates, most of which can be resolved just by attending to the varieties obscured by excessive generality.' Granted, this sounds a bit like a cheap Get out of Jail Free card, but as long as critics from within and outside the different constructionist perspectives continue to talk about 'constructionism' as a monolithic entity, this remains a valid response. My colleague certainly wasn't differentiating between types of constructionism when she represented my constructionist leanings as an unfortunate fact, and the same non-differentiated attitude can still be found in academic debates in journals and conferences. The first step in discussing the pros and cons of constructionism, then, is to be unambiguous about what assumptions exactly are subsumed under a particular use of the term 'constructionism'.

The critiques and debates have, however, established more or less stable fault lines both between different types of constructionism and between constructionisms and other approaches to social science. I will discuss some of them here.[1] First, I will outline what I think is the main bone of contention in constructionism in general, that is, the ontological claims of constructionist approaches. Figure 6.1. attempts to summarize the two positions. Its purpose is to illustrate the 'coverage' of constructionist claims, not to be the last word on the human/natural world distinction (for a discussion, see Jenkins, 2002: 111–38).

In the centre are two concentric circles representing what I call, following Jenkins (2002: 111–15), the human world and the natural world. The human world – the world that would not exist without humans – is by virtue of embodiment, among other things, part of the natural world – the world that exists independent of our ideas and discourse about it. At one end of the ontological spectrum are approaches that I call the 'world in discourse' position. In their most radical form, these claim that we can know about the human world – and the natural world, for that matter – only through discourse. Any 'reality' outside of discourse is either bracketed or denied. At the other end are approaches that I call the 'discourse in the world' position. These claim that discourse has an effect on the human world but that there are aspects of that world that are independent of us talking about it. Discourse can have a limited effect on the natural world also, through envi-

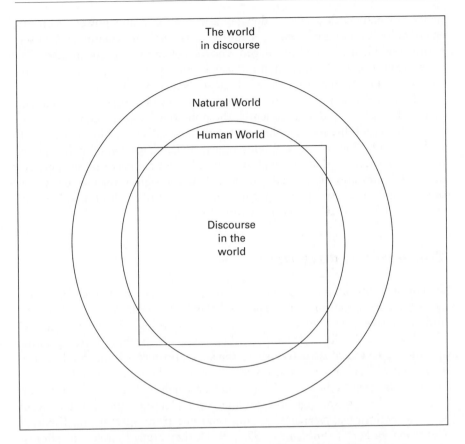

Figure 6.1   The world in discourse and discourse in the world: The coverage of constructionist claims

ronment-changing technology derived from theory, for example, but mostly the natural world keeps working regardless of our thinking and talking about it. The 'discourse in the world' position claims that we need an 'external' world in order to practise meaningful social science.

Second, I will discuss the consequences of the ontological positions on the issue of human agency. This takes us to the very premises of sociological inquiry: Is the human world produced by individuals acting in it, or do faceless structures and institutions make us what we are? Again, the varieties of constructionism have different answers. I will also discuss the how the different constructionisms address the question of social power.

The third issue concerns the putative politicization *and* apoliticization of constructionism. The issue at stake here is, on the one hand, reflexivity, that is, embracing the political embeddedness of researchers – as opposed to naïve positivist assumptions about neutral observation. On the other hand, there are two concerns about the possibility of critical, socially engaged constructionism, which dovetail with previous debates about agency and power. From an epistemological point of view if – as some constructionists claim – social scientific knowledge is not privileged knowledge, how can social scientists claim 'expertise' in any meaningful sense, if our discourse is just another discourse among others? From an ontological perspective, postmodern theorizing about the disappearance of the subject denies people – social scientists included – agency and, consequently, the potential for social change.

Finally, I will discuss how the four perspectives discussed in the book fall within the ontological and epistemological divisions presented here. Again, the main message is that although we can differentiate between perspectives on disciplinary and theoretical grounds, there are significant internal variations within the perspectives – not to mention a lot of confusion and lack of clarity about the issues raised in critical discussion.

The world in discourse

One of the most often quoted examples of the debates around the very premises of constructionism is Woolgar and Pawluch's 1985 article, where the authors introduced the much-quoted term 'ontological gerrymandering' (Woolgar and Pawluch, 1985a). In this article the authors were speaking specifically to the constructionists in the social problems tradition, but constructionists from other traditions have taken up the points as well.

The main point made by Woolgar and Pawluch is that there is an inconsistency in the way social problem scholars treat 'claims', the central concept in constructionist approaches. Taking their cue from Spector and Kitsuse's *Constructing Social Problems* ([1977]2001), they argue that constructionist theory and empirical work inspired by it treats claims-making as a social construction and an historical accomplishment, but at the same time assumes that the condition that the claims are referring to also exists 'objectively'. The basic structure of constructionist explanation, Woolgar and Pawluch argue, requires reference – even if implicit – to objective conditions:

> First, authors identify certain conditions or behaviors. Second, they identify various definitions (or claims) made about these conditions (or behaviors). Third, the authors stress the variability of the definitions vis-à-vis the constancy of the conditions to which they relate. They imply that since the condition does not vary, variations in the definition of the condition must result from the social circumstances of the definers, rather than from the condition itself (Woolgar and Pawluch, 1985a: 215).

The problem here is inconsistency: definitions of social problems made by claims-makers (that are the object of constructionist research) are relativized, that is, treated as constructions, but the condition the claims refer to are considered to be unproblematically 'true' or objectively 'out there'. Woolgar and Pawluch call this 'ontological gerrymandering', a situation where scholars selectively consider some claims about a social condition problematic, but not their own assumptions of the 'reality' of the same condition. The authors use Pfohl's (1977) paper 'The "discovery" of child abuse' as an example. The paper outlines how (parental) violence against children has changed its meaning through history, from a legitimate parental practice into modern day child abuse. Pfohl explains (Woolgar and Pawluch argue) the variations in the definition of violence against children 'by reference to socio-historical circumstances'. But, at the same time Pfohl assumes the condition to be constant. Children are being beaten; it's how we define child beating that has changed. Indeed, this is implied in the title of the paper: the placing of 'discovery' in quotation marks implies that there was nothing to be 'discovered' about 'child abuse' – the condition was always there. It is the term that was constructed, and with it the 'proper' social reaction to the condition of violence against children (Woolgar and Pawluch, 1985a: 220–221).

In philosophical usage, ontology refers to 'the study of being'. It is 'concerned with "what is", with the nature of existence, with the structure of reality as such' (Crotty, 2003: 10). But, as Michael Crotty (2003: 10–11) tells us in his textbook on social research, and as much of empirical social science assumes, most of the time we do not need to bother with ontology. 'The world' just is. This is exactly what Woolgar and Pawluch are saying constructionists are assuming when they talk about their *own* assessments of social problems conditions. The point about 'ontological gerrymandering' is that it is 'theoretically inconsistent': if the claims sociologists study are 'constructed', then, by the same logic, so are the sociologists' claims. Woolgar and Pawluch's declared purpose in drawing attention to the issue was to question whether social problems – and by extension, society in general – can be studied without 'ontological gerrymandering'. Their tentative answer is 'perhaps not', and the suggestion they offer is to think about new ways of presenting social research (Woolgar and Pawluch, 1985a: 224).

Critical responses to Woolgar and Pawluch (see below) often interpreted the article as an attack on established research and an issue of methodological refinement rather than a fundamental rethinking of sociological argumentation (Woolgar and Pawluch, 1985b). But at the same time—and partly independent of the discussion in the social problems literature—an approach that gave little or no relevance at all to the 'objective' world was gaining momentum, especially in the field of social psychology.

Edwards, Ashmore and Potter's (1995) provocative and much-cited article 'Death and Furniture' argues that relativism – under which they subsume '(social) constructionists and constructivists, deconstructionists, pragmatists, postmodernists', among others (Edwards et al., 1995: 43, fn 1) – is 'social science *par excellence*' because making statements about the 'real' world is unavoidably a rhetorical activity, and only relativism takes that aspect seriously. 'Realism' is the 'rhetoric of no rhetoric', where statements and claims that the realists favour are used to give a sense of 'out-thereness'. For the relativist constructionist this is a denial of our ultimately discourse-bound ways of making sense of the world. If Woolgar and Pawluch were unsure whether there is a way out of 'ontological gerrymandering', there is no question about it for Edwards et al. (1995: 37): 'The idea of Death and Furniture as things per se fails to resist scrutiny. There is no per se.' 'Death and Furniture' here refers to two realist arguments: it refers, first, to the idea that the physicality of furniture proves that things exist outside of discourse. To a relativist that is inherently contradictory because the act of describing a world outside discourse is itself a representation (Edwards et al., 1995: 27). Second, death – especially morally reprehensible death, like murder or genocide – is invoked as necessarily 'real' in a moral sense. Coolly detached relativism, so realists argue, denies the possibility of opposing moral evil and, in the worst case, makes evil possible. The relativist response is that realism is actually grounds for a 'rhetoric of inaction' and that the tables are easily turned: 'Are not these the folk who say we should find out the facts, discover whether some race or gender *really is* inferior on some measure, test the hypothesis, check out whether the Holocaust *really* did happen, and so on?' (Edwards et al., 1995: 35; emphasis in the original). Death and Furniture are not problems because 'there is no per se', there is nothing beyond our description of it.

Edwards et al. readily admit that the aim of their relativist project is 'negative', that is, it's function is to be critical, to be a sort of thorn on the side of naïve realist assumptions in social science, instead of offering an 'alternative reality' (1995: 40). Whether this makes for 'social science par excellence' is discussed below, but at this point it is important to point that although presented mainly as an argument about epistemology, that is, about how we can know about the world, it makes an important ontological claim as well: there simply is no 'reality' to fall back on.

In short, both critiques are saying (although addressing slightly different audiences) that constructionists (Woolgar and Pawluch) or social scientists more broadly (Edwards et al.) are *not constructionist enough*. This internal critique has created a lively discussion (especially in the sociology of social problems and social psychology), with responses ranging from a wholehearted embracing of a relativist/postmodernist position, through arguments that call for the refinement of concepts and methods, to counter-critiques of the relativist approaches.

Before moving on to the critiques of the relativist position, it should be noted that the idea of a world accessible only through discourse has also been taken up in a much more 'positive' sense than the 'fundamental critique' of the above authors suggests. Although also founded on critique of established ways of doing (in this case) psychology, Kenneth Gergen's constructionist project is much more open about presenting an 'alternative reality' that embraces more than what I have referred to as the 'human world'.

Table 6.1 Arguments for relativism

1. Inconsistency	Researchers assume that some conditions are 'real' at the same time as claims are considered constructions. Researchers' own claims are considered unproblematically 'real'.
2. 'Reality' inaccessible without discourse	We can't know about the 'world out there' without talking about it – or, in an even more radical version, the world does not exist beyond our discourse of it.

From this perspective, the 'world out there' and perceptions of that world are radically separated, with no access to former, except through discourse. It is one thing to say that the *meaning* of, say, gravity is dependent on our ways of talking about it – a position that all constructionists would happily embrace. It is another thing for me to jump out of a sixth story window and assume a safe landing because I'm shouting 'I'm not falling!' on the way down. Yet, this is the logical outcome of the 'radical' or 'extreme' (Elder-Vass, 2012: 4–6) constructionist position that posits that even the natural world is accessible only through discourse. Perhaps not surprisingly, it is this kind of constructionism that has attracted most criticism both from within and outside of the field.

Discourse in the world

For most practitioners of social science, ontology is not a big issue. Textbooks such as Crotty's *Foundations of Social Research* (2003) can tell us that ontology is not important, but they can do so only by assuming an unproblematic world 'out there', where social structures, institutions and the natural world have an existence beyond our ways of speaking about them. The more radical varieties of constructionism have challenged that assumption and brought ontology to the centre of debates about constructionism.

In this section I will discuss critiques of the 'radical' or 'extreme' position taken by the proponents of the 'world in discourse' approach. These can be divided into three main arguments. First, radical constructionism is seen as problematic because it is against everyday experience and is not free of 'ontological gerrymandering' itself. Second, critics insist that constructionism is hard-pressed to provide answers to 'why'-questions if we are limited to the study of text and talk. Most constructionisms assume that discourse transforms our ways of thinking about things, but rarely explain how this actually happens. Finally, the application of constructionist ideas in empirical research has so far overwhelmingly assumed that a world beyond discourse can be talked about and theorized about. How things have been done before is, of course, not a very good argument for what should be done in the future, but, as some critics argue, a certain realism is required in order for social science to be meaningful and valuable.

Incompatibility and inconsistency

There are two main responses to the relativist claims about theoretical inconsistencies of the 'discourse in the world' position. First, the radical relativist position seems to be incompatible with everyday experience of the natural world: theories of gravity or floating are indeed discursively constructed, but the possibility of aeroplanes taking off and boats floating requires some correlation with the natural world. Not to mention the consequences for people contemplating jumping off the sixth-floor window, as mentioned above. That something is a discursive construction does not require us to think that there is nothing beyond discourse.

The second response could be thought of as a converse 'ontological gerrymandering' argument. That is, if nothing else, relativists assume that texts and talk – discourse – exists somehow unproblematically. Yet we need a surface to inscribe our symbols on, vocal chords and sound waves to transmit our words. We could always *name* these things differently, but that does not take away the 'fact' that they are required for the communication that relativist arguments privilege. Furthermore, Gergen, in particular, talks about our making sense of the world as *dialogue*. For a dialogue to be successful, there needs to be a receiver and a respondent. So, implicitly at least, the 'world in discourse' position assumes the existence of people in dialogue (Elder-Vass, 2012: 241–2; McLennan, 2001).

Explaining the effects of discourse

A slightly different version of the ontological critique questions radical constructionisms' ability to explain *how* exactly discourse changes the human world.[2] Again, there are two variants of this critique. First, according to what could be called the 'narrow' version, we cannot know the effects of text or talk just by examining text or talk. Indeed, this constitutes what John Thompson calls a 'fallacy of internalism':

> To attempt to read off the consequences of cultural products from the products themselves is to neglect [the] ongoing activities of interpretation and assimilation; it is to speculate about the impact of these products on the attitudes and behaviour of individuals without examining this impact in a systematic way (Thompson, 1990: 105).

For Thompson, the 'systematic way' means examining the reception and appropriation of cultural products, including discourse. This reception and appropriation is an 'ongoing activity of interpretation and assimilation of meaningful content to the socially structured background characteristics of particular individuals and groups' (Thompson, 1990: 105). A good example of this is 'talking to the TV': We, as analysts, might say that the 'text' of a TV show perpetuates sexist ideas about women, for example. The show might indeed be sexist, but that doesn't mean that the sexism is not resisted by its audiences. As Talbot (2010: 227) puts it, she not only talks to the TV when sexist stereotypes are aired, she shouts and throws cushions at it as well! That audiences receive texts differently based on their social background assumes, of course, not only the 'out there' existence of individuals and groups, but also social structures that affect the interpretations that these individuals and groups are capable of making. Without this 'situatedness', meaning-making is impossible, and any claims about the effect of discourse meaningless. Critical discourse analysis, as we have seen, argues that certain linguistic forms influence our thinking in particular ways, but does not claim that discourse *defines* our thinking – lest we fall prey to the fallacy of internalism.

Second, discourse is assumed to have an effect in general and specific effects in particular, but the *mechanism* of this influence is not clear. As Elder-Vass (2011) notes, some theorizations of discourse, especially in Foucauldian vein, tend to assume rather than demonstrate the effects of discourse. This reification of discourse – the taken-for-grantedness of the causal powers of discourse – obfuscates its relation to other social practices while at the same time assuming that it has a 'more or less determinative influence on those practices' (Elder-Vass, 2011: 143). The 'world in discourse' position is hard-pressed to show how the effects of discourse can be explained. Of course, 'explanation' is often considered part of the vocabulary of 'positivist' and 'empiricist' social science irrelevant to (radical) constructionist concerns. The consequence of this is that the researcher has to take the causal influence of discourse on faith, because no mechanisms beyond discourse itself can be assumed.

Interestingly, there seems to be some profound confusion about terminology in the radical constructionist camp. Gergen (e.g. 1994: 6; 2001: 2), for example, uses 'empiricism' as a naughty word, something that constructionism opposes because (according to Gergen) it assumes an unproblematic access to the material world as a foundation for knowledge. Yet, to strictly adhere to the 'world in discourse' position means that we cannot assume any other evidence about the workings of the world except the way we talk about it. This, as Reynolds (1993: 105; Collins, 1994: 272) quite rightly notes, is a form of radical empiricism itself – only in this case discourse becomes the very foundation that radical constructionism purports to avoid.

Although it is not possible to discuss it in detail here, Dave Elder-Vass (2011; 2012) offers a compelling (ontological) realist theory of *norm circles* that takes the constructing power of discourse seriously, but also offers an explanation for its causal power. For Elder-Vass the source of the influence of discourse is in norm circles, that is, groups of people that endorse and enforce the discourses. Going back again to Berger and Luckmann's example of soup-spilling, the parents, relatives, teachers and peers constitute the expanding norm circle where the discourse of 'not-spilling-soup' is endorsed and enforced. Norm circles enable us to theorize the mechanisms through which discourse can influence and change the world, and directs our attention to the empirical questions of whether and/or which such mechanisms are actually operating in particular cases – rather than just assuming the causal influence of discourse. The main critique of the radical position here is that discourse – especially when conceptualized as 'text' – does not 'do' anything by itself, but only through people, who in turn are influenced by groups (circles) that endorse and enforce particular norms. This kind of realist view of 'discourse in the world' also has a major impact on how we conceptualize agency (see below).

Doing social science

If the argument about the ontological poverty, so to speak, of postmodernist approaches is mainly concerned about the inconsistencies and lack explanatory power of approaches that take the world to be accessible only through discourse, what I call the pragmatic argument takes a slightly different form. This kind of argument has been prominent especially in the debate about social problems theory (Best, 1993; Holstein and Miller, 1993). The pragmatic argument can be further divided into an argument from practice (how social research is done) and an argument from value (how social research should be done).

First, with a special reference to Spector and Kitsuse's (1977 [2001]) reformulation of the sociology of social problems and its further refinement by Ibarra and Kitsuse (1993), Best (1993) argues that the radically subjective (or relativist) programme of studying claims-making has not been consistently followed. The empirical research drawing from the constructionist framework continues to make reference to the world outside of discourse, whether that is in the form of institutions, interests or ideologies – essentially the same argument Woolgar and Pawluch (1985a) made. But while Woolgar and Pawluch were concerned about the theoretical consistency of the constructionist approach, Best admits the inconsistency and argues that it is a necessary component of meaningful social research – and that is reflected in the practice of social problems research. Importantly, Best notes that even if researches manage to bracket (most of) the outside world, the questions we want to ask are always affected by the assumptions we make about the world outside of discourse.

This leads to a second issue, which arises from Ibarra and Kitsuse's (1993) insistence that one toolkit – their typology of social problems rhetoric – can solve the problem of 'impure' empirical research. Yet, as Best (1993) shows, the researcher is left with a very limited number of questions to ask if the framework is strictly enforced. In fact, Best argues, most of the interesting

Table 6.2 Arguments for realism

Everyday experience and the reification of discourse	Gravity will continue to affect us, no matter how we talk about it. Also, relativists assume that discourse is unproblematically real, even if nothing else is.
Causal powers of discourse?	The effects of discourse are not dictated simply by its content (fallacy of internalism). The context of discourse enables us to analyse how discourse works through people in particular social settings.
The practice of social science	How social science has been practised and how it should be practised. Is the focus of social science society or the practices of social science itself?

and important questions cannot simply be addressed by an approach that brackets the world outside discourse. Not surprisingly, Best sees this approach as an undesirable move away from the empirical base of social research. For Best (following Gusfield, 1985: 17) – and, I would add, most social scientists working on empirical issues – the value of (constructionist) research 'is in its ability to increase our knowledge of social life' (1993: 138). This is not to say that concepts such as 'knowledge' and 'the social' are unproblematic, but the kind of 'hyper-reflexivity' advocated by the 'world in discourse' approaches turns the sociological gaze towards sociological research instead of the human world. The 'social science par excellence' turns out to be not social science in search of answers about the human world, but social science in search of answers about social science.

Agency and power

If there is one question central to sociological theory, it is the relationship between social structure and agency. The work of the classics revolved around this question, as do textbooks introducing students to the discipline. Divisions within sociology have tended to follow emphases on the structure–action continuum. So, for example, Fulcher and Scott's introductory textbook (2011: 41) explains that 'Durkheim and his followers stressed the importance of structure and saw societies as systems of structured relationships. Weber and other German sociologists tended to emphasize action and held that all social structures were, ultimately, to be seen as the outcome of human actions'. In other words: in sociology the question has been about whether a tradition privileges structure at the expense of agency, or the other way around. However, the presence of both is rarely, if ever, called into question. As we have seen in Chapter 3, one of the aims of Berger and Luckmann's sociology of knowledge is to offer an account of social life that takes both equally into account, positing structure and agency in a dialectical relationship.

Constructionism – especially perspectives inspired by Foucault and post-modern ideas – raises the question of agency in a very different sense: Constructionists of the 'world in discourse' variety seem to question the possibility of agency in the first place. The roots of this suspicion or rejection of agency lie in the critique of the individual as a knower, the individual mind as the 'origin and guarantor of meaning' (Gavey, 1989: 465). The argued 'impasse of individual knowledge' features prominently in Gergen's work, for example (1994: 1). As a consequence, 'in direct contrast to the humanist assumptions of a unified, rational *self*, poststructuralism proposes a *subject* that is fragmentary, inconsistent, and contradictory' (Gavey, 1989: 465; emphases in the original).

The problem with the concept of 'subject', as Elder-Vass (2012: 184–7) demonstrates, is the variety of ways it is used by different authors – and sometimes in a single author's work. More problematic, however, is the way in which some theorizations seem to do away with the idea of agency altogether. For these approaches – to simplify a complex argument somewhat – being a subject means *being subjected* to a discourse that valorizes the individual as a knower and a free decision maker, but which actually only masks the fact that our sense of the self is (purely) a product of discourse itself. To put it differently: we do not perform discourse; discourse performs us (Fairclough, 1992: 45; Elder-Vass, 2012: 187–9; see Chapter 4).

Perhaps not surprisingly some of the most heated debates about constructionism and agency have involved feminist thinkers, for whom agency is not only a matter of theoretical interest, but a key point in assessing how to change the world (see below). Political action is part of Judith Butler's project as well – her criticism points to the heteronormativity of feminist thinking about the subject, as we have seen above – but her (and others') apparent denial of agency has problematic consequences for the feminist project, as other influential feminists have argued (see Elder-Vass, 2012: 190–194). As Holmes (2007: 102) puts it from a sociological perspective:

> Certainly sociologists might be sympathetic to [Butler's] distrust of 'voluntarism', by which she means assumptions that human beings can do whatever they choose. Clearly, sociology is often an exercise in destroying illusions of individual choice by revealing the determining power of social structures on people's lives. But it is very difficult to eschew voluntarism while trying to promote some vision of agency.

The political consequences of disappearing agency are discussed in the next section, but the issue dovetails with the issue of power. Power is a key part of the vocabulary of the more postmodern approaches as well, but if there is 'no doer behind the deed' as Butler, for example, seems to suggest (Holmes, 2007: 102), it becomes difficult to think of ways in which individuals could be agents of social change. Moreover, if power is ubiquitous but not exercised by anyone, identifying sources of power and ideology (as per the critical tradition discussed in Chapter 5) becomes impossible. Although in some of his work Foucault seems to suggest that subjects are capable of resistance (Elder-Vass, 2012: 189), it is not clear how this can be reconciled with the view that discourse 'forms' subjects rather than the other way around.

The issue of disappearing agency and its implications for the concept of power is a problem specific to variations of the 'world in discourse' position. But even approaches that do not deny or diminish agency have been criticized for not paying enough attention to power. Thus we have, for example, Giddens (1979: 267, n.8) commenting that *The Social Construction of Reality* 'completely lacks a conception of the critique of ideology'. As Giddens and others (Turner, 2008) have argued, Berger and Luckmann are more interested in 'order' than the ways in which individuals' role in the human world is affected by power. Elsewhere, in the context of social problems research, Heiner (2002: 10) argues that while popular constructions of social problems are indeed the focus of interest, constructionists have mostly ignored elite interests, the ways in which these influence claims, and ways that they are made to pass as 'common' interests. To sum up: agency is constrained and enabled by power. The critiques point to varieties of constructionism which use one concept without paying sufficient attention to the other.

The progressive and conservative politics of constructionism

There are two ways of thinking about the 'politics of constructionism': In the first, narrow sense, constructionism – especially the social psychology perspective – has been critical of the objectivity claims of traditional social science. The constructionists' aim has been to show that 'positivist' science is as embedded in ideology as any social practice. According to this view there is no such thing as 'apolitical' (social) science, and instead of clinging to necessarily unsatisfactory attempts at objectivity, social scientists should embrace relativism. The debates around this position are debates about the reflexivity of the social sciences, that is, the role of interests and the 'human factor' in the production of scientific knowledge. As such, they are not the main focus of this section, although the discussion overlaps with the broader sense of 'politics' in constructionism. This second sense refers to the moral questions raised by the relativism that some constructionisms espouse. That is, 'how can we say, for example, that certain groups are oppressed, if these "groups" and their "oppression" are constructions which can have no greater claim to truth than any other?' (Burr, 1998: 14). Although it is only possible here to scratch the surface and introduce the positions (for fuller accounts and attempts at solving the moral relativism problem, see Parker, 1998), the discussion around the possibility of political action nicely demonstrates how the different debates intersect and how moral questions necessarily dovetail the above debates about ontology and agency.

Liberation as discursive achievement

Stephen Sanderson, who is highly critical of constructionism (which, for him, consists of symbolic interactionism and ethnomethodology), summarizes the political attraction of ethnomethodology in a way that can be applied to constructionism more broadly as well.

> It is interesting that ethnomethodologists are often political radicals, and a good many of them are, politically speaking, Marxists. Why should this be? The reason may be that ethnomethodology is attractive to such people because it has a simple agenda for dramatic social change: get people to alter their social definitions by showing them that their existing definitions are somehow flawed. Rebuild the world through cognitive change. (Sanderson, 2001: 27).

Whether one agrees with Sanderson's assessment about ethnomethodologists' Marxism is one thing – Reynolds (1993: 105) explicitly denies it, and many Marxists would find ethnomethodology antithetical to their endeavours– but he is very likely right about the attractions of constructionism. The idea of a contingent world is a powerful one for those seeking to change it. Vivien Burr, speaking from the social psychology perspective, confirms this:

> When I first began to read about social constructionist ideas in the late 1980s, I was attracted, as I believe were many others, by the liberatory promise of its anti-essentialism. […] If what we take ourselves and others to be are constructions and not objective descriptions, and if it is human beings who have built these constructions, then it is (at least in principle) possible to reconstruct ourselves in ways which might be more facilitating for us (Burr, 1998: 13).

Burr goes on to add that 'it becomes possible to think not only of individuals re-construing aspects of themselves, but of re-thinking whole social categories' (Burr, 1998: 13). As Shakespeare (1998), among others, shows, constructionism has had an especially important impact on issues that have been traditionally taken as matters of biology and nature. Gender, disability and sexuality are examples of issues where the inadequacy of women, disabled people, and homosexuals is considered part of a natural order: women are the 'weaker sex', disabled people physically inadequate, and homosexuality a pathology, a case of physiological and psychological degeneration (Shakespeare, 1998: 170–71). As Kate Millett puts it: 'patriarchy has a tenacious or powerful hold through its successful habit of passing itself off as nature' (1971: 58, quoted in Shakespeare ,1998: 170).

Constructionism enables seeing these issues (among others, such as race) in a very different light: not only is the idea of 'inadequacy' a matter of social definition, but the categories of women, disabled people and homosexuals are products of historical categorization processes themselves. Edwards et al. (1995: 34) express the same idea in the broadest possible sense:

> Reality can serve as rhetoric for inaction (be realistic ... face the facts ... come off it ... you can't walk through rocks ... you can't change reality, human nature, market forces ... it's just the way things are ... life isn't fair). It is a familiar kind of argument against change, against action, against open-ended potentiality of any kind. Reality is given, perceived, out-there and constraining. (Emphases in the original.)

In a way the academic 'fate' of Berger and Luckmann's constructionism – and their own assessment of its fate – is indicative of the ways in which constructionism has been appropriated as a vehicle for 'liberation'. Berger has more than once bemoaned how the idea and terminology of 'construction' was taken as a licence for an 'orgy of ideology and utopianism' (Berger, 2011: 92), that is, the emergence of academic Marxism, feminism and other movements, while the actual point of *The Social Construction of Reality* and its phenomenological approach was forgotten. As we have seen in the chapters above, the language of construction did gain widespread currency in the social sciences around and after Berger and Luckmann's book. Nevertheless, Berger has been persistent about the uses that he thinks the idea of social construction can and cannot be applied to. In a reply to a suggestion that the application of Berger's ideas to research have benefited from a growing gender-awareness (Heelas and Woodhead, 2001: 70–71), he replied: 'I will politely dissent from the proposition that this calls for a "gendered" perspective' (Berger, 2001: 193). There is no doubt that the idea of construction has a strong attraction to approaches that seek to highlight issues of power inequality (class, gender, sexuality, ethnicity, race, and so forth) – even if the constructionist field has been internally divided between those who, in a classic Weberian sense of detached analysis, want to keep 'ideology' out of the objective practice of social science, and those who, in the name of reflexivity, prefer to wear their politics on their sleeve.

The unintended conservatism of constructionism

Not everyone shares Berger's views on the (mis)appropriation of the concept of social construction. For Berger, 'constructionism' became synonymous with radical politics, but for others, the possibility of constructionist politics in the first place is suspect. From this point of view constructionism – at least in its postmodern forms – is actually conservative because it does not recognize the ontological constraints of social structure and power nor provide the individual with insufficient agency for political action (see, e.g., Callinicos, 1989). Speaking specifically on the reflexivity issue, Parker (1998: 1) comments on the dual consequences of radically relativist constructionisms:

> At the same time as deconstruction, discourse theory, pragmatism and postmodernism cut away the positivist ground from beneath traditional psychology and relativize their claims about the nature of human nature, these theoretical currents also relativize the truth claims of the critics and sabotage principled resistance to abuses of power in the discipline.

More broadly conceived, those claiming that constructionism is inherently conservative argue that it is so because it conflates ontology and epistemology, as in the 'world in discourse' position. Combining the idea that the world is accessible only through discourse with a hyper-reflexivity where no discourse has a privileged status results in an 'inability to commit to a political position' (Willig, 1998: 92). 'Ideological critique', as Gergen defines it, has indeed 'broken from its Marxist moorings', when the point of critique is to 'remove the truth claim from contention by shifting the site of consideration from the claim itself to the ideological or motivational from which it derives' (Gergen, 1994: 36, 37). 'Critique' in this sense becomes detached from any reference to truth or accuracy of claims. The consequence of this is, as Merttens (1998: 61) puts it: 'Without a faith that one way of working may be fairer, more democratic, less cruel, more egalitarian than another, *and* that it may be faithfully so described, we are unable to commit ourselves to any course of action or, indeed, to offer assistance to others' (emphasis in the original). This echoes the discussion on agency discussed above. It is also no accident that calls for a more moderate constructionism have been voiced by groups such as feminists and socialists with an active agenda for social change. As I will discuss in the next chapter, constructionist ideas have not been the sole property of academic discourse, but have also been appropriated in 'applied' forms, such as social work.

Berger stands out from the crowd as an explicit 'conservative' representative of constructionism (see Turner, 2008: 496), but the critique of constructionism as potentially conservative obviously applies to some of the other perspectives discussed here as well. While CDA (at least in its early versions by Fairclough) is explicitly political and progressive, the 'world in discourse' versions of the sociology of social problems and social psychology are susceptible to the critique of conservatism, despite their often explicit claims to the contrary.

A plurality of constructionisms

Constructionism has many varieties, that much we know by now. In the preceding chapters the main point of distinction has been disciplinary background: we have discussed Berger and Luckmann's sociology of knowledge, the sociology of social problems, social psychology, and critical discourse analysis. But the disciplinary perspectives are also internally diverse, as the critiques in this chapter demonstrate. While it is difficult, if not impossible, to impose a 'correct' reading on often ambiguous theoretical texts, or pigeonhole diverse fields of inquiry into neat categories, my aim in this section is to examine how the issues raised by the critical debates apply to each perspective. My focus will be on the ontological positioning and/or debates within a perspective, but I will discuss the other issues if they have featured prominently in the disciplinary debates.

Berger and Luckmann's ideas put forth in *The Social Construction of Reality* are, of course, different from the other perspectives because they do not – despite being widely referred to – constitute a 'school' or 'tradition' in any coherent sense. Quite the contrary, their often ambiguous formulations have enabled widely varied readings. On the one hand, their approach is considered 'idealist' because it seems to suggest that 'reality is conferred upon [phenomena] by our coming to believe that they are real' (Elder-Vass, 2012: 236; see Archer, 1995: 13). On the other hand, the 'world' of Berger and Luckmann 'looks a great deal like the ordinary mundane world' (Collins, 1994: 272) and 'their approaches to cultural phenomena had a clear understanding of the concreteness of everyday reality' (Turner, 2000: xv; see Hacking, 1999: 25). The same difficulty of interpretation is reflected in critiques of agency and structure in Berger's work on religion specifically. Again, on the one hand, Berger is accused of putting too much emphasis on the individual at the cost of ignoring constraining structures (Wuthnow, 1986: 138–9). On the other hand, he is criticized for structural determinism, that is, for suffocating agency (Douglas, 1982: 17). In the world of academic discourse, authors cannot control how their work is interpreted any more than, say, journalists can control how their stories are interpreted around the breakfast table. In addition, scholars with long careers often change their minds – Berger's views on secularization being a case in point – and write contradictory things, which makes pinning down the thoughts of even one person difficult. Yet, as little as it might affect the prevailing perceptions of *The Social Construction of Reality*, Berger himself has been adamant that if 'constructivism' means postmodern theory, 'Luckmann and I have felt constrained to say repeatedly, "We are not constructivists"' (Berger, 2011: 95). Indeed, 'as to the most radical formulation of this "postmodernism"– that nothing really exists but the various "narratives" – this corresponds very neatly with a definition of schizophrenia, when one can no longer distinguish between reality and one's fantasies' (Berger, 2011: 95).

Of all the perspectives discussed here, constructionist sociology of social problems has been most explicitly divided between 'strict' and 'contextual' constructionists. Although Spector and Kitsuse's constructionist reformulation of the object of social problems – claims-making instead of conditions – 'sub-jectivized' the field, the constructionist study of social problems, as presented by its adherents and as discussed above in Chapter 3, assumed an unproblematic world 'out there'. This (often implicit) position is a classic example of 'discourse in the world'. Inspired by the critical scrutiny that started with Woolgar and Pawluch's influential article (1985a) on 'ontological gerrymandering', some constructionist scholars turned increasingly (although not always consistently) towards postmodernist ideas from European literary and cultural studies on the one hand, and ethnomethodological considerations on the other (Ibarra and Kitsuse, 1993; Lynch, 2008; Schneider, 2008). Ibarra and Kitsuse's (1993) reformulation attempted to scrap the last remaining references to objective conditions and suggested an approach that would concentrate solely on texts and rhetoric. The people who did the claims-making, and who were at the centre of the symbolic interactionist tradition from which constructionist social problems research sprang, disappeared when text and discourse took their place. According to critics, the price of theoretical consistency was too high: not only was an approach that bracketed all 'reality' outside discourse untenable, it also did away with agency (Best, 1993). Ten years after Ibarra and Kitsuse's 'postmodernist' reformulation of social problems research, Best (2003: 149) was confident enough to say that 'the qualms about ontological gerrymandering that arose in the 1980s and threatened to impede the perspective's development have been put aside'. The field is in flux, but the fault lines between 'strict' (postmodern, ethnomethodological) and 'contextual' (realist, interactionist) seem to be established as more or less permanent features (Best, 1993; 2003).

Positioning constructionist approaches to psychology within the critiques discussed in this section is difficult and apt not to do justice to the diversity within the perspective. Yet, foregrounding the postmodernist tendencies of constructionist social psychology is justified in the broader framework of constructionisms discussed in this book. Although some of the foundational works (Potter and Wetherell, 1987, for example) cannot be said to represent a radical 'world in discourse' approach (despite sometimes being written by people associated with it), discursive and/or narrative psychology has been and continues to be (Lock and Strong, 2010) identified with postmodernist ideas more than any of the other perspectives. It is unclear what the actual effect of the more radical positions has been on empirical research in (social) psychology, but if Dave Elder-Vass is to be believed, postmodernism's influence still lingers in debates about social theory, although the heyday of postmodernism is over – indeed, despite the 'fact' that postmodernism 'is dead' (Elder-Vass, 2012: 4).

Finally, although originally identified mainly with the work of Norman Fairclough, critical discourse analysis has become an important subfield of discourse studies, which in turn bridge disciplines ranging from sociology to linguistics. Of all the traditions discussed in this book, CDA has been most explicit about the dialectical nature of social life. Discourse is the key object of research, but it is always considered in relation to broader social formations. Nevertheless, critics from within the perspective have been concerned about the balance of textual and social analysis in CDA. As Richardson (2007: 28) puts it:

> Unfortunately however, despite claims to the contrary, the dominant approach in CDA has been to separate language use from language users; to treat discourse as a thing that *in itself* can include or exclude, reproduce social inequalities or effect social change. This line of argument has, to a greater extent, been encouraged by the dominance of a linguistically based analysis in CDA, which (whilst acknowledging the socially constituted character of discourse) has tended to start from 'the text' and to 'argue forward' to imputed social effects. Indeed, Fairclough (1992: 6) has gone as far as to suggest that contemporary social changes are 'constituted to a significant extent by changes in language practices'. Such an approach slides precariously close to an Idealistic conception of social reality, in contrast to Fairclough's declared commitment to Marxist social theory. (Emphasis in the original.)

Marxist social theory features much less prominently in Fairclough's later work, but even so, he has explicitly identified with critical realism (Fairclough et al., 2004) – perhaps as a response to the more postmodern ways of conceiving 'constructionism'. Indeed, ethical and political critique – 'challenging the features that contribute to the perpetuation of structured inequalities' – that is at the heart of CDA, can '*only* take place when texts and their (ideological) claims are "analysed against the facts – the reality" of social practices and relations of power more specifically' (Richardson, 2007: 42, quoting Jones, 2001: 245; emphasis in the original). CDA remains strongly committed to the idea of 'discourse in the world'.

Conclusion

In this chapter I have discussed debates within constructionism and critical perspectives from non-constructionist positions. I identified ontology as the key dividing factor in constructionist debates, with 'radical' approaches at the one end claiming that we can only access 'the world' through discourse, and 'moderate' or 'contextual' approaches arguing that discourse influences 'the world' but also that there are aspects of the world that exist independently of our thinking or communicating about them. A corollary of the ontology debate is the question of agency: What is the role of people in social change? How does power affect agency? Again, the fault lines are drawn between approaches that see agency as something enacted or performed anew in every communication event (the 'world in discourse' approach), and approaches that argue that people's positions in the social structure influences their possibilities of taking part in the discursive construction of the human world (the 'discourse in the world' approach). Closely dovetailing the agency issue are questions regarding the possibilities for political action that different constructionist ideas enable – or prohibit. Finally, I discussed how the debates about ontology, agency, power, and politics have been featured in the four different perspectives. What emerges is a pluralism of constructionisms, where the perspectives are often internally diverse, but also occupy more or less stable positions regarding the above debates.

Social Constructionisms and the Study of the Human World

7

The previous chapters have discussed the basic idea of social construction, a choice of disciplinary traditions that apply the idea of construction in some form and the critiques and responses to constructionist ideas. These will have hopefully given you, the reader, tools to navigate the sometimes-thick jungle of constructionisms. There are, however, some further issues that, while not central for understanding constructionist ideas as such, warrant discussion, especially in light of applying constructionist ideas to empirical research. That is, I think, after all the point of all (meta)theorizing about the social world. The aim of this chapter is, then, to discuss how constructionism can be best understood in relation to practical research. In doing so I will stray into broader questions of social-scientific research design. Finally, I will discuss constructionism as a source for practical social action.

Epistemology, theory, methodology?

What does it mean to apply constructionism in empirical research? So far I have discussed this only through the 'case studies' into exemplary uses of a particular perspective, but I have said very little about how we could or should think about the role of constructionism in the research process. In other words, what exactly is constructionism in terms of research design? Is it an epistemology, a theory, methodology, or something else? Unfortunately, the literature is not always helpful in finding straightforward answers. As we have seen above, Crotty (2003: 10–11) is happy to tell the readers of his guide to social research that we can safely leave questions of ontology to philosophers. Yet, Elder-Vass's (2012) important reassessment argues for a 'social ontology' approach to processes of construction.

What about, epistemology, then? Consider the following statements:

> Constructionism is an *epistemology* embodied in many theoretical perspectives, including symbolic interactionism as this is generally understood. An

epistemology, as we have already seen, is a way of understanding and explaining how we know what we know. (Crotty, 2003: 3; emphasis in the original).

[For some scholars] constructionism is neither an epistemology nor a sociological substitute for epistemology but a technique or a mode of analysis (Velody and Williams, 1998: 4).

When planning this section, I had in mind first of all students in the social sciences struggling with the 'theoretical framework' (or similar) chapter required for their dissertations and essays. Can constructionism be considered as a theory, theoretical framework, or a 'theoretical perspective' (Crotty, 2003)? There are varying ideas about what theory and theorizing are (for a discussion and a narrow view, see Sanderson, 2001; cf. Crotty, 2003: 7–8), but for our purposes it is safe to say that constructionism is something rather broader than a theory. Many theories specific to a discipline and focusing on particular phenomena employ constructionist ideas, but they tend to be in the form of 'constructionist theory of such and such' rather than plain 'constructionism'. Thus we have constructionist sociology of social problems, for example – the only one of the perspectives discussed above that has developed constructionist ideas into a recognizable disciplinary theory. On the other hand, there are many fields of inquiry that employ the idea of social construction in some form, without actually having a coherent theory around the idea, or using it in a borrowed, 'secondary' way. For example, in my main field of expertise, the sociology of religion, 'construction' is regularly invoked, but mainly in two senses: (a) as a metatheoretical question about how the category 'religion' is constructed in everyday life and by scholars alike, and (b) as a variation of broader identity theory, where a religious identity is said to be 'constructed' (but see Beckford, 2003).

Finally, could constructionism be called a methodology, that is, something 'mediating' between epistemological and theoretical approaches and the choice of actual research methods (Crotty, 2003: 7)? This is especially relevant when considering discourse analysis, which is sometimes understood narrowly as a method, or at least a methodology, as Crotty (2003: 5) does. We know by now, of course, that there is much more going on in discourse analysis than methodological rethinking. It is fair to say that adopting a discourse-analytical and, by extension, a constructionist, approach will obviously affect both one's choice of epistemology and the particular method 'toolkit' suitable for research. Nevertheless, constructionism is more than methodology.

A 'technique' sounds too, well, technical to apply to constructionism in any sensible way, but I think a 'mode of analysis', referred to by Velody and Williams above, comes close to a useful concept. Somewhat banally, I would prefer to call constructionism an 'approach'. This is because such a broad concept encompasses all of the above questions: ontology, epistemology, theory and methodology. Few empirical studies are explicit about these aspects, leading to the confusion that characterizes the term 'constructionism'. My contention is that, minimally, any study employing 'constructionism' should be explicit about its ontological commitments, lest the concept become empty. Empirical studies are required to anchor themselves in the theoretical and conceptual discussions of the discipline and/or its subfields, but if 'constructionism' is invoked, that is not yet sufficient. Instead, it would be a service to the scholars, their readers and constructionism as an approach to be explicit about *what kind* of constructionism a particular study espouses.

Asking the right questions

If constructionism is best conceived as an 'approach', encompassing ontology, epistemology, theory and methodology, how does it – practically speaking – enter into doing research? As a preliminary, and without going into the tiresome and mostly useless debate about quantitative versus qualitative social science, let me just remark that constructionist approaches lend themselves 'naturally' to qualitative research. Therefore – without dismissing the idea that 'construction' *might* be employed in counting social phenomena in innovative ways – when I speak of the research process, I have qualitative research in mind.

The key element of any study is the research question. The importance of research questions cannot be overemphasized, especially with regard to dissertations and theses (see White, 2009). The point of good social science is always to do more than just describe people or social phenomena. 'What' –questions are a *part* of social scientific enquiry, but the best social science aims for more: to uncover patterns and, if possible, to point causal connections. The question, then, is: *what kind of questions can constructionist research ask?*

The answer that has become almost standard in the literature has two varieties. First, from a sympathetic perspective, constructionism should focus on 'how' –questions, because the idea of construction implies a process. To study ethnic identity, for example, means studying how particular groups produce an ethnic group identity and how individuals within the group appropriate these identities. This would also have to take into account the external constructions (media, etc.) of the group and assess how those influence the internal constructions (see, for example, Jenkins, 2008). The 'world in discourse' position also sees how-questions as the most fundamental. Reference to a context where people's interactions could be explained – *why* they said something – is meaningless, because there is no context beyond discourse, as we have learned above (see Silverman and Gubrium, 1994).

The second, much less sympathetic, standard answer is that constructionism has to stick with 'how'-questions because it is unable to answer 'why'-questions, that is, questions that aim to demonstrate a causal connection between phenomena (Sanderson, 2001). One of the reasons some critics say constructionism can never be properly called a 'theory' is that it cannot *explain* social phenomena, which 'proper' (narrowly conceived) theory is supposed to do. For these critics constructionism is forever relegated to the 'fluffy' world of *under-standing*, where how-questions rule.

Asking the right questions brings us again – on an abstract level, at least – to the issue of context. Those referred to as 'contextual constructionists' do not shy away from why-questions because they see reference to contexts of discourse as necessary. This is also the position of 'realist constructionists' such as Elder-Vass (2012; see Gorski, 2004). Even some of those sympathetic to the 'world in discourse' position have conceded that why-questions are possible if 'context' is understood as something constructed in interaction as well – although how-questions should always precede why-questions. Thus:

> [O]ne's initial move should be to pay close attention to how participants locally produce or enact contexts for their interaction [...] we can fruitfully move on to broader why questions to 'explain' the place in everyday life of structural or cultural constraints, on the one hand, and expectations or identities, on the other (Silverman and Gubrium, 1994: 180).

The theoretical and methodological discussion about the principles of social-scientific research cannot be covered here, so suffice it to say that I don't think why-questions should be left to quantitative research alone. The important thing is to acknowledge the limitations of one's arguments when asking and answering why-questions. Textual data cannot produce generalizations in the way numerical can, but it can point out patterns and mechanisms. We can, for example, discern relatively stable differences in the way in which working-class and middle-class people talk about social (in)equality. That does not give us averages or medians to use for policy-making, but it does tell us how class positions affect the ways we talk about ourselves and others. At the end of the day, developing research questions is a multifaceted process (White, 2009), but constructionism, as an approach in the broad sense, is an important influence in that process.

Constructionisms and engaged social science

Much, if not most, constructionist research has an emancipatory aim (Hacking, 1999: 2). Sometimes this can refer to emancipation from the conventions of mainstream research, contributing to the development of individual academic disciplines or the broader field of social science. But sometimes constructionist research reaches beyond the academia with an aim to change the ways in which we think about something and, possibly, how we act and make policy. As we have seen in the politics and constructionism section above, some key figures in the field, notably Peter Berger, have disdained the conflation of constructionism and political activism. Other approaches, namely those of the 'world in discourse' variety, have run into a paradoxical situation where activism is advocated but undermined at the same time by denying agency and extra-discursive influences on social issues (see above). Yet, social change is 'on the menu' for most constructionisms. In this last section I will discuss how the calls for action can reach beyond the walls of the proverbial ivory tower of academia – how academic constructionism can become applied constructionism (Miller, 2003).

There are three ways of thinking about constructionist practice in the 'real' life. These represent different levels of engagement with constructionist ideas. First, at the level of individuals and families, for example, there are forms of therapy that employ constructionist ideas. Lock and Strong (2010: 349) discuss 'narrative' therapy, which aims to 'help people resolve problems by discovering new ways of *storying* their situation' (my emphasis). They go on:

> These stories construct the person's understanding of who they are and frame their interpretations of what's troubling them. The role of the therapist is to help the client find an alternative and preferable story, one that enables them to repudiate and escape their problem-saturated situation (Lock and Strong, 2010: 349).

Miller (2003: 239) in turn discusses 'solution-focused brief therapy', which, instead of problem-solving, 'stresses building alternatives to clients' problems by socially constructing goals and resources that clients might use in changing their lives'.

While therapy is regulated by governments and professional associations in many countries, social scientists of other persuasions can be and have been active in other arenas of social life. On the second level, constructionism has been used not only to analyse the construction of social problems, but to create 'social problem movements'. The process of claims-making (Spector and Kitsuse, 2001), the types of rhetoric (Ibarra and Kitsuse, 1993) and the audiences of claims (Loseke, 1999) can be analysed with an aim to create effective campaigns about issues that people feel need changing. Speaking about social problem *movements* can give the impression of spontaneous uprisings later organized into a mass phenomenon, like the civil rights movement in the USA. Claims-making is more often, however, done within the 'social problems industry' (politics, lobbies, organizations, media, and so on; see Loseke, 1999: 29–32). News-making criminology, discussed above, is an attempt to bridge the academic/applied divide by scholars targeting the media in order to change hegemonic views on crime that misuse statistics, for example, and reproduce a culture of fear that disproportionately targets particular minorities (Barak, 1994b; Glassner, 2009). Miller (2003: 243–5) argues that applied constructionist practitioners should treat claims-makers (if not such themselves) as clients, creating a responsible relationship. While readily applicable to therapy and 'narrative urban planning', where urban planning is approached as a story, it is perhaps less suitable for cases like news-making criminology, where social action springs from an ethical and political commitment rather than a service relationship.

Miller (2003: 250) points to a key challenge in practising constructionism:

On the one hand, social problems claims are appeals for social change that sometimes have potentially radical implications for selected groups and institutions in society. But, on the other hand, it is unusual for potentially radical social problems campaigns to produce radical institutional change. Social problems claims-making is seldom a springboard for revolution.

While it is true that 'social problems claims-makers who cannot persuasively argue that their preferred solutions can be built within existing or acceptable institutions risk having their claims disputed by others' (Miller, 2003: 250), from a different perspective there is (a) no problem in the above statement and (b) Miller's own language of 'clientism' is a source of the failure to produce radical change. From a broadly Marxist and CDA perspective, claims, i.e. public discourse, are always in competition with other claims. Claims compete for visibility in the first place and then against alternative claims. Being 'disputed' is not a problem as such; being ignored or silenced (hegemony) is. Again, from a critical Marxist perspective, Miller's proposition that constructionist practitioners treat themselves as experts offering services to clients reproduces capitalist ideology – and the accompanying inequalities – itself.

At the third level, then, we can identify constructionist practices that aim at wide-ranging changes in thinking that have an impact on everyday practices. Although obviously much rarer than successful 'campaigns' by more narrowly defined social problems movements, many of the major 'liberations' of the previous century have included an element of discursive rethinking. This is perhaps most apparent in feminism. After changing from a suffrage movement fighting for women's right to vote into a diverse set of ideas and practices around gender equality, one of its lasting impacts has been championing inclusive language use. Sexism is embedded in the language we use, and one of the more visible ways of combating it has been the now-widespread practice of gender-neutral terms (for example, chairperson vs. chairman). The role of language in gender equality continues to be hotly debated and the appropriation of gender-inclusive language in administration or the media frequently evokes accusations of 'political correctness' (Talbot, 2010: 224–42). If gender-inclusive language amounts to a revolution, it is an on-going one. Nevertheless, applying what Fairclough (1995: 219–32) calls Critical Language Awareness in education, for example, can have a wide-ranging impact. If we learn to use non-disparaging terms for social groups (women, ethnic and sexual minorities, etc.), we can learn to think and talk differently about them. That, as constructionisms of all varieties attest, is the key to social change.

Conclusion

In this chapter I have discussed how to make sense of constructionisms in the framework of empirical research. I examined different ways of conceptualizing constructionism – as ontology, epistemology, theory and methodology – and suggested that constructionism is best characterized, somewhat banally, as an 'approach' that includes all of the above aspects. As a minimum, I argued that constructionist research should be explicit about its ontological premises. I also briefly discussed the kinds of questions that constructionist approaches best lend themselves to. Although how-questions have traditionally been considered the bread and butter of constructionist research, I suggested that discourse-analytical work can answer why-questions as well, *if* the ontology of the approach permits reference to extra-discursive structures and processes. Finally, I discussed how constructionism has been and can be put to use outside the academy. I identified three levels of engagement with society: therapy, social movement organization and broader, possibly 'revolutionary' changes in the ways which we think about things. I offered feminists' work on inclusive language practices as an example of wide-ranging social change. Changing the way we think and talk about things is a form of social action that, so constructionists believe, can have effects on how we legislate about these things and how we encounter these things in everyday interaction, for example. This is how the human world is made. Constructed, if you will.

Notes

1 The World We Make: The Idea of Social Construction

1. This example is inspired by Harold Garfinkel's 'experiments' discussed in Chapter 2.
2. 'The human world' refers 'simply, to the world with humans in it, the world that is made by humans, the world as seen from a human point of view [...] to a world peopled in the first place by individuals, but only and always doing things collectively, with other humans, and always identified, at least in large part, by their collective attachments to other humans' (Jenkins, 2002: 64). Although I adopt Jenkins's terminology in this chapter, I continue to use 'society' and 'culture' in describing the traditions of constructionism, especially when these terms appear in them.
3. Foucault is most often referred to as a representative of 'poststructuralism', an academic current that emphasized the role of language in constituting the structures that earlier 'structuralists' claimed were the source of our language use. Postmodernism is a broader cultural current, including art and literature, but the two overlap in many ways. Many argue that Foucault actually ignored or at least downplayed the role of individual actors and social interaction to the point where discourse becomes an all-encompassing structure that defines what we are as subjects. Conflicting interpretations notwithstanding, Foucault's influence on the use of 'discourse' as a social scientific concept cannot be overemphasized.
4. Suicide pacts have, however, been documented especially in the US (see Gaines, 1991).
5. As mentioned, the debate around Kuhn's ideas continues. The following discussion is not intended as an uncritical endorsement of all of Kuhn's arguments, but rather as a simplified example of how (scientific) knowledge is socially produced (for discussion see, for example, Sharrock and Read, 2002; Kukla, 2000; Hacking, 1999).
6. Notoriously, Kuhn uses the word 'paradigm' in at least two different senses (Kuhn, 1996: 175; Bird, 2000: 67). For the sake of simplicity, I am following Barnes and using 'paradigm' to denote an 'accepted problem-solution in science' (Barnes, 1982: xiv).
7. The concept of paradigm has also sometimes been used to describe conceptual and theoretical development in the social sciences. This, however, is problematic because 'knowledge' in the social sciences is usually understood differently from the natural sciences. It is therefore not possible for any one theoretical view to

become paradigmatic in the social sciences the same way that happens in the natural sciences (Sharrock and Read, 2002: 126–130).

8. The exception is Ludwig Wittgenstein, who has inspired many anthropologists and sociologists (see Barnes, 1982: 35).

9. Hacking (1999: 43) notes, however, that there is very little in Kuhn's text about actual interaction between scientists, the focus being on ideas. What later became known as sociology of scientific knowledge (SSK) has filled this vacuum with empirical studies of 'normal' and 'revolutionary' science.

10. Again, as Sharrock and Read (2002: 174–5) remind us, Kuhn himself has denied association with views that claim that 'reality' is socially constructed. What he prefers to talk about is socialization. Nevertheless, his work has inspired much more radical constructionist views on scientific knowledge.

2 The Construction of Everyday Life: The Sociology of Knowledge

1. Both Weber and Durkheim's theories can be interpreted in a myriad of ways (see, for example, Giddens, 1979; Collins, 1988) and not all agree on the Action (Weber) vs. Structure (Durkheim) perspective presented here. Therefore, the current juxtaposition is made mostly for the purpose of emphasizing the two different approaches to the study of the 'social'.

2. Berger and Luckmann's discussion of primary socialization has been influenced, especially, by George Herbert Mead (1934), from whom the concept of 'significant others,' for example, is taken (Berger and Luckmann, 1967: 195n6, 196n10, 197n22, 198n36).

3. For a classic statement on this issue, see Paul Willis' *Learning to Labour* (1979) and *Profane Culture* (1978). Some scholars have suggested that contemporary mass mediated popular culture has narrowed the differences between youth of different social classes. However, this is largely dependent on the social context, and even in the media-saturated societies of the West, class status continues to have an effect on educational and occupational careers, if not so much on 'style'.

4. In *The Social Construction of Reality* the authors use the term *universe-maintenance*, but in his later work Berger (1973) has substituted the term *world-maintenance*. I have opted for the latter because I think it better expresses the process of subjective legitimation in the here and now (Berger and Luckmann, 1967: 22) of everyday reality – the 'world' – whereas universe-maintenance refers more strongly to legitimation on the level of symbolic universes.

5. All references to *The Sacred Canopy* in this chapter refer to the pages of the British edition published as *The Social Reality of Religion* (Berger, 1973).

6. Berger uses the term theodicy in an original way. In a more theological sense, theodicies can be defined as 'specific explanations or justifications of suffering in a world believed to be ruled by a morally good God' (Green, 1987: 431). For Berger, however, theodicies are the basic building blocks of meaning, even if they do not promise an end to suffering: 'It would [...] be misleading to consider theodicies only in terms of their "redemptive" potential. Indeed, some theodicies carry no promise of "redemption" at all – except for the redeeming assurance of meaning itself' (Berger, 1973: 66).

3   The Making of the Dark Side of Society: Social Problems as Social Constructions

1.   For examples, see Stallings, 1990; Best, 1991; Gamson et al., 1992; Fishman, 1998; Surette, 1998; Critcher, 2003.
2.   For examples, see Fuller and Myers, 1941; Lemert, 1967; Blumer, 1971; Mauss, 1975; Spector and Kitsuse, 2001.
3.   The *Crime in England and Wales 2010/11* report can be found online at http://www.homeoffice.gov.uk/publications/science-research-statistics/research-statistics/crime-research/hosb1011/hosb1011?view=Binary   (Accessed   18 December 2013).

4   Constructing the Self: Social Psychology, Discourse and Postmodernism

1.   This, of course, is the idea behind Ferdinand Tönnies' differentiation between *Geheimschaft* and *Gesellschaft*, and Emile Durkheim's conceptualization of 'mechanical' and 'organic' solidarity. See Chapter 3.
2.   Butler (2002, loc 350–56) comments, insightfully I think, that 'there is a sense in which French postmodernism is a true successor to the surrealist movement, which also tried to disrupt supposedly "normal" ways of seeing things'.
3.   The same could be argued about skin colour, of course, especially when the diversity of people is reduced to a binary 'white' versus 'non-white', as has historically often been the case.
4.   In this context 'strength' should be understood not only as the ability to lift a heavy weight once (as our consumer workout culture would have us think), which someone with larger body mass possibly could do, but also stamina.
5.   Interestingly, looking at empirical studies on verbal ability within a constructionist framework, I found none that consistently applied the postmodern agenda. See Chapter 6.

5   The Power of Construction: Critical Discourse Analysis

1.   In a narrow sense, 'critical theory' refers specifically to a group of theorists referred to as the Frankfurt School, including Theodor Adorno, Max Horkheimer and Jurgen Habermas. Here, however, the term is used in a more inclusive sense to denote all approaches that focus on power relations in society.
2.   The term 'Critical Constructionism' has been used earlier in a quite different sense than the one suggested here. Robert Heiner's book *Social Problems: An Introduction to Critical Constructionism* draws mainly from American social problems theory (see Chapter 4) and combines that with Marxist ideas of power (Heiner, 2002; see Hjelm, 2004). Although the concept of power as developed by Marx and thinkers influenced by him is common to both approaches, 'critical constructionism' in the sense I am using it here draws from the combination of

Foucauldian social theory, discourse analysis, and the critical use of the concept of ideology rather than the constructionist tradition of social problems research.

3.   Chouliaraki and Fairclough (1999: 32) do, however, use the Bourdieusian term 'constructivist structuralism' to describe the epistemological underpinnings of critical social science and CDA in particular.

6   Constructionisms and Critique

1.   For a comprehensive critique of constructionism from a realist perspective, see Elder-Vass, 2012. For older critiques that often address only one or two of the perspectives discussed above, see, e.g., Reynolds, 1993; Parker, 1998; Sanderson, 2001; see also Volume 32, Issue 3 (1985) of the journal *Social Problems*.

2.   I am here referring only to discourse, whereas Elder-Vass's (2012) account of social ontology covers and differentiates between culture, language, discourse and knowledge.

References

Abercrombie, N. 'Knowledge, Order, and Human Autonomy', in James Davison Hunter and Stephen C. Ainlay (eds) *Making Sense of Modern Times: Peter L. Berger and the Vision of Interpretive Sociology* (London and New York: Routledge and Kegan Paul, 1986), pp. 11–30.

Agger, B. *Critical Social Theories: An Introduction.* 2nd edition (Boulder, CO: Paradigm Publishers, 2006).

Akers, R. *Criminological Theories: Introduction, Evaluation, and Application.* 3rd Edition (Los Angeles: Roxbury, 2000).

Archer, M.S. *Realist Social Theory: The Morphogenetic Approach* (Cambridge: Cambridge University Press, 1995).

Arminen, I. *Therapeutic Interaction: A Study of Mutual Help in the Meetings of Alcoholics Anonymous* (Helsinki: The Finnish Foundation for Alcohol Studies, 1998).

Barak, G. 'Media, Society, and Criminology', in Gregg Barak (ed.) *Media, Process and the Social Construction of Crime: Studies in Newsmaking Criminology* (New York and London: Garland Publishing, 1994a), pp. 3–45.

Barak, G. 'Newsmaking Criminology: Reflections on the Media, Intellectuals, and Crime', in Gregg Barak (ed.) *Media, Process and the Social Construction of Crime: Studies in Newsmaking Criminology* (New York and London: Garland Publishing, 1994b), pp. 237–64.

Barker, E. 'The Cult as a Social Problem', in T. Hjelm (ed.) *Religion and Social Problems* (New York: Routledge, 2011), pp. 198–212.

Barnes, B. *T.S. Kuhn and Social Science* (New York: Columbia University Press, 1982).

Bauman, Z. *Thinking Sociologically* (Cambridge: Polity Press, 1990).

Becker, H.S. *Outsiders: Studies in the Sociology of Deviance* (New York: The Free Press of Glencoe, 1991[1963]).

Becker, H.S. 'The Chicago School, So-Called', *Qualitative Sociology* 22:1 (1999), 3–12.

Beckford, J.A. *Social Theory and Religion* (Cambridge: Cambridge University Press, 2003).

Bellah, R. 'Civil Religion in America', *Daedalus* 21:1 (1967), 1–21.

Berger, P.L. *Invitation to Sociology: A Humanistic Perspective* (Garden City, NY: Anchor Books, 1963).

Berger, P. L. *The Social Reality of Religion* (Harmondsworth: Penguin, 1973). Originally published in 1967 as *The Sacred Canopy.*

Berger, P. L. *Facing Up to Modernity* (New York: Basic Books, 1977).

Berger, P. L. 'Epilogue', in James Davison Hunter and Stephen C. Ainlay (eds) *Making Sense of Modern Times: Peter L. Berger and the Vision of Interpretive Sociology* (London and New York: Routledge and Kegan Paul, 1986), pp. 221–235.

Berger, P. L. 'Reflections on the Twenty-Fifth Anniversary of "The Social Construction of Reality"', *Perspectives* 15:2 (1992) 1–4.

Berger, P. L. (ed.) *The Desecularization of the World: Resurgent Religion and World Politics* (Grand Rapids, MI: Eerdmans, 1999a).

Berger, P. L. 'The Desecularization of the World: A Global Overview', in Peter L. Berger (ed.) *The Desecularization of the World: Resurgent Religion and World Politics* (Grand Rapids, MI: Eerdmans, 1999b), pp. 1–18.

Berger, P. L. 'Postscript', in Linda Woodhead with Paul Heelas and David Martin (eds) *Peter L. Berger and the Study of Religion* (London: Routledge, 2001), pp. 189–198.

Berger, P. L. 'Whatever Happened to Sociology?', *First Things* 126 (October 2002) 27–29.

Berger, P. L. *Adventures of an Accidental Sociologist: How to Explain the World Without Becoming a Bore* (Amherst, NY: Prometheus Books, 2011).

Berger, P.L. and Berger, B. *Sociology: A Biographical Approach*. 2nd, expanded edition (New York: Basic Books, 1975).

Berger, P.L., Berger, B. and Kellner, H. *The Homeless Mind: Modernization and Consciousness* (New York: Vintage, 1973).

Berger, P. L. and Luckmann, T. *The Social Construction of Reality: A Treatise in the Sociology of Knowledge* (Garden City, NY: Anchor Books, 1967 [1966]).

Best, A. *Prom Night: Youth, Schools, and Popular Culture* (New York: Routledge, 2000).

Best, J. '"Road Warriors" on "Hair-Trigger Highways": Cultural Resources and the Media's Construction of the 1987 Highway Shootings Problem', *Sociological Inquiry* 61:3 (1991), 327–45.

Best, J. 'But Seriously Folks: The Limitations of the Strict Constructionist Interpretation of Social Problems', in James A. Holstein and Gale Miller (eds) *Reconsidering Social Constructionism* (New York: Aldine deGryuter, 1993), pp. 129–47.

Best, J. (ed.) *Images of Issues: Typifying Contemporary Social Problems* (New York: Aldine deGryuter, 1995a).

Best, J. 'Typification and Social Problems Construction', in Joel Best (ed.) *Images of Issues: Typifying Contemporary Social Problems* (New York: Aldine deGryuter, 1995b), pp. 3–10.

Best, J. 'The Diffusion of Social Problems', in Joel Best (ed.) *How Claims Spread: The Cross-National Diffusion of Social Problems* (New York: Aldine de Gruyter, 2001), pp. 1–18.

Best, J. 'Staying Alive: Prospects for Constructionist theory', in James A. Holstein and Gale Miller (eds) *Challenges and Choices: Constructionist Perspectives on Social Problems* (New York: Aldine de Gruyter, 2003), pp. 133–52.

Best, J. *Social Problems* (New York: W. W. Norton & Co., 2007).

Bettelheim, B. *The Uses of Enchantment: The Meaning and Importance of Fairy Tales* (New York: Vintage Books, 1977[1975]).

Bhaskar, R. 'Afterword', in John Shotter *Conversational Realities: Constructing Life Through Language* (London: Sage, 1993), pp. 185–7.

Bird, A. *Thomas Kuhn* (Princeton: Princeton University Press, 2000).

Bloor, M. and Wood, F. *Keywords in Qualitative Methods: A Vocabulary of Research Concepts*. (London: Sage, 2006).

Blumer, H. *Symbolic Interactionism* (Englewood Cliffs, NJ: Prentice-Hall, 1969).

Blumer, H. 'Social Problems as Collective Behavior', *Social Problems* 18 (Winter) (1971), 298–306.

Bourdieu, P. *Culture/Power/History* (Princeton, NJ: Princeton University Press, 1994), p. 163.

Bourdieu, P. and Passeron, J-C. *Reproduction in Education, Society and Culture*. 2nd edition (London: Sage, 1990). Originally published in 1970 as *La Reproduction*.

Bromley, D.G. 'The Satanic Cult Scare', *Society* 28:4 (1991), 55–66.

Bruce, S. *Religion in the Modern World: From Cathedrals to Cults* (Oxford: Oxford University Press, 1996).

Bulmer, M. *The Chicago School of Sociology: Institutionalization, Diversity, and the Rise of Sociological Research* (Chicago: University of Chicago Press, 1984).

Burr, V. *Introduction to Social Constructionism* (London: Routledge, 1995).

Burr, V. 'Overview: Realism, Relativism, Social Constructionism and Discourse', in Ian Parker (ed.) *Social Contructionism, Discourse and Realism* (London: Sage, 1998), pp. 13–25.

Burr, V. *Social Constructionism*. 2nd edition (London: Routledge, 2003).

Butler, J. *Gender Trouble* (London: Routledge, 1990).

Calhoun, G. *Critical Social Theory: Culture, History and the Challenge of Difference* (Cambridge, MA: Blackwell, 1995).

Callinicos, A. *Against Postmodernism: A Marxist Critique* (Cambridge: Polity, 1989).

Campbell, C. 'A New Age Theodicy for a New Age', in Linda Woodhead with Paul Heelas and David Martin (eds) *Peter L. Berger and the Study of Religion* (London: Routledge, 2001), pp. 73–84.

Carey, J.T. *Sociology and Public Affairs: The Chicago School* (Beverly Hills: Sage, 1975).

Chermak, S. 'The Presentation of Drugs in the Media: The News Sources Involved in the Construction of Social Problems', in Gary W. Potter and Victor E. Kappeler (eds.) *Constructing Crime: Perspectives on Making News and Social Problems* (Prospect Heights, Illinois: Waveland Press, 1998), pp. 161–192.

Chouliaraki, L. and Fairclough, N. *Discourse in Late Modernity* (Edinburgh: Edinburgh University Press, 1999).

Chiricos, T., Eschholz, S. and Gertz, M. 'Crime, News and Fear of Crime: Towards an Identification of Audience Effects', in G.W. Potter and V.E. Kappeler (eds) *Constructing Crime: Perspectives on Making News and Social Problems* (Prospect Heights, Illinois: Waveland Press, 1998), pp. 295–315.

Cohen, S. *Moral Panics and Folk Devils*. 3rd edition. (New York: Routledge, 2002[1972]).

Collins, R. *Theoretical Sociology* (San Diego: Harcourt Brace Jovanovich, 1988).

Collins, R. *Four Sociological Traditions* (New York: Oxford University Press, 1994).

Critcher, C. *Moral Panics and the Media* (Buckingham: Open University Press, 2003).

Crotty, M. *The Foundations of Social Research: Meaning and Perspective in the Research Process* (London: Sage, 2003).

Dayan, D. and Katz, E. 'Articulating Consensus: The Ritual and Rhetoric of Media Events', in Jeffrey C. Alexander (ed.) *Durkheimian Sociology: Cultural Studies* (Cambridge: Cambridge University Press, 1988), pp. 161–186.

Dor, D. 'On Newspaper Headlines as Relevance Optimisers', *Journal of Pragmatics* 35:5 (2003), 695–721.

Douglas, M. 'Passive Voice Theories in Religious Sociology', *Review of Religious Research* 21:1 (1979), 51–61.

Durkheim, É. *Suicide* (New York: The Free Press, 1979). Originally published in 1897 as *Le Suicide*.

Durkheim, É. *The Rules of Sociological Method* (New York: The Free Press, 1982). Originally published in 1895 as *Les Règles de la méthode sociologique*.

Durkheim, E. *The Division of Labour in Society* (Basingstoke: Palgrave, 1984). Originally published in 1893 as *De la division du travail social*.

Durkheim, É. *The Elementary Forms of Religious Life* (New York: The Free Press, 1995). Originally published in 1912 as *Les Formes élémentaires de la vie religieuse*.

Edelman, M. *Constructing the Political Spectacle* (Chicago: University of Chicago Press, 1988).

Edwards, D., Ashmore, M, and Potter, J. 'Death and Furniture: The Rhetoric, Politics and Theology of Bottom Line Arguments Against Relativism' *History of the Human Sciences* 8:2 (1995), 25–49.

Edwards, D. and Potter, J. *Discursive Psychology*. (London : Sage, 1992).

Elder-Vass, D. 'The Causal Power of Discourse' *Journal for the Theory of Social Behaviour* 41:2 (2011), 143–160.

Elder-Vass, D. *The Reality of Social Construction* (Cambridge: Cambridge University Press, 2012).

Ellis, B. 'The Devil-Worshippers at the Prom: Rumor-Panic as Therapeutic Magic', *Western Folklore* 49:1 (1990), 27–49.

Erikson, K. T. *The Wayward Puritans: A Study in the Sociology of Deviance* (New York: John Wiley and Sons, 1966).

Fairclough, N. *Language and Power* (London: Longman, 1989).

Fairclough, N. *Discourse and Social Change* (Oxford: Polity Press, 1992).

Fairclough, N. *Media Discourse* (London: Arnold, 1995a).

Fairclough, N. *Critical Discourse Analysis* (London: Longman, 1995b).

Fairclough, N. *Analysing Discourse: Textual Analysis for Social Research* (London: Routledge, 2003).

Fairclough, N., Jessop, B. and Sayer, A. 'Critical Realism and Semiosis', *Journal of Critical Realism* 5:1 (2002), 2–10.

Finch, J. 'Coming to Your Senses', in A. Cheuse and L. Alvarez (eds) *Writers Workshop in a Book* (San Francisco: Chronicle Books, 2007), pp. 86–94.

Fine, G.A. (ed.) *A Second Chicago School: The Development of a Postwar American Sociology* (Chicago: University of Chicago Press, 1995).

Fishman, M. 'Crime Waves as Ideology', in G.W. Potter and V.E. Kappeler (eds) *Constructing Crime: Perspectives on Making News and Social Problems* (Prospect Heights: Waveland Press, 1998), pp. 53–72.

Foucault, M. *The History of Sexuality 1: The Will to Knowledge* (London: Penguin, 1978[1976]).

Foucault, M. *Discipline and Punish: The Birth of the Prison* (New York: Vintage Books, 1995[1975]).

Franz, P. and Warren, D.I. 'Neighborhood Action as a Social Movement: Perspectives on Trends in the United States and West Germany', *Comparative Political Studies* 20:2 (1987), 229–246.

Fulcher, J. and Scott, J. *Sociology*. 4th edition (Oxford: Oxford University Press, 2011).

Fuller, R. C. and Myers, R. R. 'The Natural History of a Social Problem', *American Sociological Review* 6:3 (1941), 320–8.

Fuller, S. 'The Reflexive Politics of Constructionism Revisited', in I. Velody and R. Williams (eds) *The Politics of Constructionism* (London: Sage, 1998), pp. 83–99.

Gaines, D. *Teenage Wasteland: Suburbia's Dead End Kids* (New York: Pantheon, 1991).

Gamson, W.A., Croteau, D., Hoynes, W. and Sasson, T. 'Media Images and the Social Construction of Reality', *Annual Review of Sociology* 18 (1992), 373–93.

Gans, H. J. 'Reopening the Black Box: Toward a Limited Effects Theory', *Journal of Communication* 43:4 (1993), 29–35.

Garfinkel, H. 'A Conception of, and Experiments with, 'Trust' as a Condition of Stable Concerted Actions', in O.J. Harvey (ed.) *Motivation and Social Interaction* (New York: Ronald Press, 1963), pp. 187–238.

Garfinkel, H. *Studies in Ethnomethodology* (Englewood Cliffs, NJ: Prentice-Hall, 1967).

Gavey, N. 'Feminist Poststructuralism and Discourse Analysis', *Psychology of Women Quarterly* 13:4 (1989), 459–475.

Gergen, K. J. 'The Social Constructionist Movement in Modern Psychology', *American Psychologist* 40:3 (1985), 266–75.

Gergen, K. J. *The Saturated Self: Dilemmas of Identity in Contemporary Life* (New York: Basic Books, 1991).

Gergen, K. J. *Realities and Relationships: Soundings in Social Construction* (Cambridge, MA: Harvard University Press, 1994).

Gergen, K. J. *An Invitation to Social Construction* (London: Sage, 1999).

Gergen, K. J. *Social Construction in Context* (London: Sage, 2001).

Gergen, K. J. and Gergen, M. 'Social Construction and Psychological Inquiry' in J.A. Holstein and J.F. Gubrium (eds) *Handbook of Constructionist Research* (New York: The Guilford Press, 2008), pp. 171–186.

Gergen, M. and Gergen, K. J. *Social Construction: A Reader* (London: Sage, 2003).

Gergen, K. J. and Wortham S.E.F. 'Social Construction and Pedagogical Practice', in K.J. Gergen (ed.) *Social Construction in Context* (London: Sage, 2001), pp. 115–136.

Giddens, A. *Central Problems in Social Theory: Action, Structure and Contradiction in Social Analysis* (London and Basingstoke: Macmillan, 1979).

Giddens, A. 'Living in a Post-Traditional Society', in U. Beck, A. Giddens and S. Lash. *Reflexive Modernization: Politics, Tradition and Aesthetics in the Modern Social Order* (Stanford, CA: Stanford University Press, 1994), pp. 56–109.

Glassner, B. *The Culture of Fear*. 10th anniversary edition (New York: Basic Books, 2009).

Goode, E. and Ben-Yehuda, N. *Moral Panics: The Social Construction of Deviance* (Oxford: Blackwell, 1994).

Gorski, P. 'The Poverty of Deductivism: A Constructive Realist Model of Sociological Explanation', *Sociological Methodology* 34:1 (2004), 1–33.

Gramsci, A. *Selections from the Prison Notebooks* (London: Lawrence and Wishart, 1971).

Gray, J. *Men are from Mars, Women are from Venus* (New York: HarperCollins, 1992).

Green, R.M. 'Theodicy', in *The Encyclopedia of Religion*, Vol. 14 (New York: Macmillan, 1987), pp. 430–441.

Gusfield, J.R. 'Theories and Hobgoblins', *SSSP Newsletter* 17 (Fall 1985): 16–18.

Gusfield, J.R. *Symbolic Crusade: Status Politics and the American Temperance Movement*. 2nd edition (Urbana and Chicago: University of Illinois Press, 1986[1963]).

Hacking, I. *The Social Construction of What?* (Cambridge, MA: Harvard University press, 1999).

Hall, S., Critcher, C., Jefferson, T., and Clarke, J. and Roberts, B. *Policing the Crisis: Mugging, the State, and Law and Order* (Basingstoke: Macmillan, 1978).

Halpern, D.F. *Sex Differences in Cognitive Abilities.* 4th edition (New York: Psychology Press, 2012).

Hammond, P.E. 'Religion in the Modern World', in James Davison Hunter and Stephen C. Ainlay (eds) *Making Sense of Modern Times: Peter L. Berger and the Vision of Interpretive Sociology* (London and New York: Routledge and Kegan Paul, 1986), pp. 143–158.

Harré, R. 'Foreword', in Ian Parker (ed.) *Social Contructionism, Discourse and Realism* (London: Sage, 1998), pp. xi–xii.

Heelas, P. and Woodhead, L. 'Homeless Minds Today?', in Linda Woodhead with Paul Heelas and David Martin (eds) *Peter L. Berger and the Study of Religion* (London: Routledge, 2001), pp. 43–72.

Heelas, P. and Woodhead, L. with Seel, B. and Szerszynski, B. and Tusting, K. *The Spiritual Revolution: Why Religion is Giving Away to Spirituality* (Oxford: Blackwell, 2005).

Heiner, R. *Social Problems: An Introduction to Critical Constructionism* (New York and Oxford: Oxford University press, 2002).

Heiskala, R. 'Sosiaalinen konstruktionismi', in Risto Heiskala (ed.) *Sosiologisen teorian nykysuuntauksia* (Helsinki: Gaudeamus, 2000), pp. 146–172.

Heritage, J. *Garfinkel and Ethnomethodology* (Cambridge: Polity Press, 1984).

Herrnstein Smith, B. *Scandalous Knowledge: Science, Truth and the Human* (Durham, NC: Duke University Press, 2006).

Hervieu-Léger, D. 'The Twofold Limit of the Notion of Secularization', in Linda Woodhead with Paul Heelas and David Martin (eds) *Peter L. Berger and the Study of Religion* (London: Routledge, 2001), pp. 112–125.

Hjelm, T. 'Social Problems: An Introduction to Critical Constructionism.' Book review of Robert Heiner, *Social Problems: An Introduction to Critical Constructionism*, *Acta Sociologica*, 47:1 (2004), 97–8.

Hjelm, T. 'Driven by the Devil: Popular Constructions of Adolescent Satanist Careers', in J.R. Lewis and J. Aagaard Petersen (eds) *The Encyclopedic Sourcebook of Satanism* (Amherst, NY: Prometheus Books, 2008).

Hjelm, T., Bogdan, H., Dyrendal A. and Petersen, J. 'Nordic Satanism and Satanism Scares: The Dark Side of the Secular Welfare State', *Social Compass* 56:4 (2009), 515–529.

Hollinger, R. *Postmodernism and the Social Sciences: A Thematic Approach* (Thousand Oaks, CA: Sage, 1994).

Holmes, M. *What is Gender? Sociological Approaches* (London: Sage, 2007).

Holstein, J.A. and Gubrium, J.F. 'The Constructionist Mosaic', in J.A. Holstein and J.F. Gubrium (eds) *Handbook of Constructionist Research* (New York: The Guilford Press, 2008), pp. 3–10.

Holstein, J.A. and Miller, G. 'Reconsidering Social Constructionism', in James A. Holstein and Gale Miller (eds) *Reconsidering Social Constructionism* (New York: Aldine deGryuter, 1993), pp. 5–23.

Holstein, J.A. and Miller, G. (eds) *Challenges and Choices: Constructionist Perspectives on Social Problems* (New York: Aldine de Gruyter, 2003).

Hunter, J.T. and Ainlay, S.C. (eds) *Making Sense of Modern Times: Peter L. Berger and the Vision of Interpretive Sociology* (London: Routledge, 1986).

Ibarra, P. and Kitsuse J.I. 'Vernacular Constituents of Moral Discourse: An Interactionist Proposal for the Study of Social Problems' in James A. Holstein and gale Miller (eds) *Reconsidering Social Constructionism* (New York: Aldine deGryuter, 1993), pp. 25–58.

Jenkins, P. *Intimate Enemies: Moral Panics in Contemporary Britain* (New York: Aldine de Gruyter, 1992).

Jenkins, P. 'The Ice Age: The Social Construction of a Drug Panic', in Gary W. Potter and Victor E. Kappeler (eds.). *Constructing Crime: Perspectives on Making News and Social Problems* (Prospect Heights: Waveland Press, 1998), pp. 137–160.

Jenkins, R. *Foundations of Sociology: Towards a Better Understanding of the Human World* (Basingstoke: Palgrave, 2002).

Jenkins, R. *Social Identity*. 3rd edition (Abingdon: Routledge, 2008).

Jones, P.E. 'Cognitive Linguistics and Marxist Approach to Ideology', in René Dirven, Bruce Hawkins and Esra Sandikcioglu (eds) *Language and Ideology. Volume I: Theoretical Cognitive Approaches* (Amsterdam: John Benjamins, 2001), pp. 227–251.

Kitsuse, J.I. and Spector, M. 'Toward a Sociology of Social Problems: Social Conditions, Value-Judgments, and Social Problems', *Social Problems* 20:4 (1973), 407–19.

Kitsuse, J.I. and Spector, M. 'Social Problems and Deviance: Some Parallel Issues', *Social Problems* 22:5 (1975), 584–594.

Kuhn, T.S. *The Structure of Scientific Revolutions*. 3rd edition (Chicago and London: The University of Chicago Press, 1996[1962]).

Kukla, A. *Social Constructivism and Science* (London: Routledge, 2000).

Laqueur, T. *Making Sex: Body and Gender from the Greeks to Freud* (Harvard: Harvard University Press, 1990).

LaFontaine, J.S. *Speak of the Devil: Tales of Satanic Abuse in Contemporary England* (Cambridge: Cambridge University Press, 1998).

Larrain, J. 'Ideology and Hegemony', in J. Scott (ed.) *Sociology: The Key Concepts* (London: Routledge, 2006), pp. 85–8.

Lemert, E. M. *Human Deviance, Social Problems, and Social Control* (Englewood Cliffs, NJ: Prentice-Hall, 1967).

LeVine, M. *Heavy Metal Islam: Rock, Resistance, and the Struggle for the Soul of Islam* (New York: Random House/Three Rivers Press, 2008).

Lock, A. and Strong, T. *Social Constructionism: Sources and Stirrings in Theory and Practice* (Cambridge: Cambridge University Press, 2010).

Lofquist, W. S. 'Constructing "Crime": Media Coverage of Individual and Organizational Wrongdoing', in Gary W. Potter and Victor E. Kappeler (eds) *Constructing Crime: Perspectives on Making News and Social Problems* (Prospect Heights: Waveland Press, 1998), pp. 241–261.

Lorber, J. 'Constructing Gender: The Dancer and the Dance', in J.A. Holstein and J.F. Gubrium (eds) *Handbook of Constructionist Research* (New York: The Guilford Press, 2008), pp. 531–544.

Loseke, D. R. *Thinking about Social Problems: An Introduction to Constructionist Perspectives* (New York: Aldine De Gruyter, 1999).

Luckmann, T. *The Invisible Religion* (New York: Macmillan, 1967).

Luckmann, T. 'Berger and his Collaborator(s)', in Linda Woodhead with Paul Heelas and David Martin (eds) *Peter L. Berger and the Study of Religion* (London: Routledge, 2001), pp. 17–25.

Lynch, M. 'Ethnomethodology as a Provocation to Constructionism', in James A. Holstein and Jaber F. Gubrium (eds) *Handbook of Constructionist Research* (New York, NY: The Guilford Press, 2008), pp. 715–31.

Lyotard, J.-F. (1984) *The Postmodern Condition: A report on Knowledge.*

Minneapolis: The University of Minnesota Press. Originally published in 1979 as *La condition postmoderne: rapport sur le savoir.*

Macdonell, D. *Theories of Discourse: An Introduction* (Oxford: Basil Blackwell, 1986).

McLennan, G. '"Thus": Reflections on Loughborough Relativism' *History of the Human Sciences* 14: 3 (2001), 85–101.

Macridis, R. *Contemporary Political Ideologies: Movements and Regimes.* 5th edition (New York: HarperCollins, 1992).

Mannheim, K. *Ideology and Utopia: An Introduction to the Sociology of Knowledge* (San Diego: Harvest, 1936).

Marx, K. *Selected Writings in Sociology and Social Philosophy.* Bottomore, T.B. and Rubel, M. (eds.) (Harmondsworth: Penguin, 1961).

Mauss, A.L. *Social Problems as Social Movements* (Philadelphia: Lippincott, 1975).

Mead, G. H., *Mind, Self, and Society: From the Standpoint of a Social Behaviorist* (Chicago: The University of Chicago Press, 1934).

Merttens, R. ¨What Is to be Done? (With Apologies to Lenin!)', in Ian Parker (ed.) *Social Constructionism, Realism and Discourse* (London: Sage, 1998), pp. 59–74.

Miller, G. 'Getting Serious About an Applied Constructionism of Social Problems', in James A. Holstein and Gale Miller (eds) *Challenges and Choices: Constructionist Perspectives on Social Problems* (New York: Aldine de Gruyter, 2003), pp. 236–254.

Miller, G. and Holstein, J.A. (eds) *Constructionist Controversies: Issues in Social Problems Theory* (New York: Aldine de Gruyter, 1993).

Millett, K. *Sexual Politics* (New York: Avon Books, 1971).

Mills, S. *Feminist Stylistics* (London: Routledge, 1995).

Mills, S. *Discourse.* 2nd edition (London: Routledge, 2004).

Molyneux, J. *Will the Revolution be Televised? A Marxist Analysis of the Media* (London: Bookmarks, 2012).

Mäkelä, K. et al. *Alcoholics Anonymous as Mutual Self-Help Movement: A Study in Eight Societies* (Madison, WI: University of Wisconsin Press, 1996).

Oakley, A. *Sex, Gender and Society* (London: Temple Smith, 1972).

Ollman, B. *Alienation: Marx's Conception of Man in Capitalist Society.* 2nd edition (Cambridge: Cambridge University Press, 1976).

Parker, I. (ed.) *Social Contructionism, Discourse and Realism* (London: Sage, 1998).

Payne, M. 'Social Construction in Social Work and Social Action', in A. Jokinen, K. Juhila and T. Pösö (eds) *Constructing Social Work Practices* (Aldershot: Ashgate, 1999).

Pfohl, S.J. 'The "Discovery" of Child Abuse' *Social Problems* 24:3 (1977), 310–323.

Portney, K.E. and Berry, J.M. 'Mobilizing Minority Communities: Social Capital and Participation in Urban Neighborhoods', *American Behavioral Scientist* 40:5 (1997), 632–644.

Potter, G.W and Kappeler V.E. 'Introduction', in G.W Potter and V.E. Kappeler (eds) *Constructing Crime: Perspectives on Making News and Social Problems* (Prospect Heights: Waveland Press, 1998), pp. 1–24.

Potter, J. *Representing Reality: Discourse, Rhetoric, and Social Construction* (London: Sage, 1996).

Potter, J. and Wetherell, M. *Discourse and Social Psychology: Beyond Attitudes and Behaviour* (London: Sage, 1987).

Putnam, R.D. *Bowling Alone: The Collapse and Revival of American Community* (New York: Simon and Schuster, 2000).

Reinarman, C. and Levine H.G. 'The Crack Attack: America's Latest Drug scare, 1986–1992', in Joel Best (ed.) *Images of Issues: Typifying Contemporary Social Problems* (New York: Aldine deGryuter, 1995), pp. 147–86.

Restivo, S. and Croissant, J. 'Social Constructionism in Science and Technology Studies', in J.A. Holstein and J.F. Gubrium (eds) *Handbook of Constructionist Research* (New York: The Guilford Press, 2008), pp. 213–229.

Reynolds, L. *Interactionism: Exposition and Critique.* Third edition (Dix Hills, NY: General Hall, 1993).

Richardson, J.E. *Analysing Newspapers: An Approach from Critical Discourse Analysis* (Basingstoke: Palgrave Macmillan, 2007).

Roof, W.C. Spiritual Marketplace: *Baby Boomers and the Remaking of American Religion* (Princeton, NJ: Princeton University Press, 1999).

Rubington, E. and Weinberg M.S. (eds.) *The Study of Social Problems: Seven Perspectives* (New York and Oxford: Oxford University Press, 1995).

Sacco, V.F. 'Media Constructions of Crime', *Annals of the American Academy of Political and Social Science* 539 (1995), 141–154.

Sanderson, S. K. *The Evolution of Human Sociality: A Darwinian Conflict Perspective* (Lanham, MD: Rowman and Littlefield, 2001).

Sasson, T. *Crime Talk: How Citizens Construct a Social Problem* (New York: Aldine De Gruyter, 1995).

Scheufele, D. A. and Tewksbury, D. 'Framing, Agenda Setting, and Priming: The Evolution of Three Media Effects Models', *Journal of Communication* 51:1 (2007), 9–20.

Schneider, J. 'Saving Social Construction: Contributions from Cultural Studies', in James A. Holstein and Jaber F. Gubrioum (eds) *Handbook of Constructionist Research* (New York, NY: The Guilford Press, 2008), pp. 733–51.

Schutz, A. *The Phenomenology of the Social World* (London: Heinemann, 1980). Originally published in 1932 as *Die Sinnhafte Aufbau der Sozialen Welt.*

Schutz, A. and Luckmann, T. *The Structures of the Life-World* (Evanston, IL: Northwestern University Press, 1973).

Schutz, A. and Luckmann, T. *The Structures of the Life-World*, Vol. 2 (Evanston, IL: Northwestern University Press, 1989).

Scott, J. *Power* (Cambridge: Polity Press, 2001).

Scott, J. 'Power', in J. Scott (ed.) *Sociology: The Key Concepts* (London: Routledge, 2006), 127–31.

Scott, S. 'The Definition of the Situation', in J. Scott (ed.) *Sociology: The Key Concepts* (London: Routledge, 2006), 51–3.

Shakespeare, T. 'Social Constructionism as a Political Strategy, in Irving Velody and Robin Williams (eds) *The Politics of Constructionism* (London: Sage, 1998), pp. 168–81.

Sharrock, W. and Read, R. *Kuhn: Philosopher of Scientific Revolutions* (Cambridge: Polity Press, 2002).

Shotter, J. *Conversational Realities: Constructing Life through Language* (London: Sage, 1993).

Silverman D. *A Very Short, Fairly Interesting and Reasonably Cheap Book about Qualitative Research.* (London: Sage, 2007).

Silverman, D. and Gubrium J.F. 'Competing Strategies for Analyzing the Contexts of Social Interaction', *Sociological Inquiry* 64:2 (1994), 179–198.

Smart, N. *The World's Religions.* 2nd edition (Cambridge: Cambridge University Press, 1998).

Smolej, M. and Kivivuori, J. 'The Relation between Crime News and Fear of Violence', *Journal of Scandinavian Studies in Criminology and Crime Prevention* 7:2 (2006), 211–227.

Spector, M. and Kitsuse J.I. 'Social Problems: A Re-Formulation', *Social Problems* 21:2 (1973), 145–59.

Spector, M. and Kitsuse, J. I. *Constructing Social Problems* (New Brunswick, NJ: Transaction Publishers, 2001 [1977]).

Stallings, R.A. 'Media and the Social Construction of Risk', *Social Problems* 37:1 (1990), 80–95.

Suoninen, E. 'Näkökulma sosiaalisen todellisuuden rakentumiseen', in A. Jokinen, K. Juhila and E. Suoninen, *Diskurssianalyysi liikkeessä* (Tampere: Vastapaino, 1999), pp. 17–36.

Surette, R. 'A Serendipitous Finding of a News Media History Effect', in Gary W. Potter and Victor E. Kappeler (eds) *Constructing Crime: Perspectives on Making News and Social Problems* (Prospect Heights: Waveland Press, 1998), pp. 265–74.

Talbot, M. *Language and Gender*. 2nd edition (Cambridge: Polity, 2010).

Tannen, D. *You Just Don't Understand* (London: Virago, 1991).

Thompson, J.B. *Studies in the Theory of Ideology* (Cambridge: Polity Press, 1984).

Thompson, J.B. *Ideology and Modern Culture* (Stanford: Stanford University Press, 1990).

Thompson J.B. *The Media and Modernity* (Cambridge: Polity Press, 1995).

Tong, R. *Feminist Thought: A Comprehensive Introduction* (London: Routledge, 1992 [1989]).

Tracy, S.W. and Acker, C.J. *Altering American Consciousness: The History of Alcohol and Drug Use in the United States, 1800–2000* (Amherst: University of Massachusetts Press, 2004).

Turner, B.S. 'Preface to the Second Edition', in Bryan S. Turner (ed.) *The Blackwell Companion to Social Theory* (Oxford: Blackwell, 2000), pp. xiii–xviii.

Turner B.S. 'The Constructed Body', in James A. Holstein and Jaber F. Gubrioum (eds) *Handbook of Constructionist Research* (New York, NY: The Guilford Press, 2008), pp. 493–510.

van Dijk, T.A. *News as Discourse* (Hillsdale, NJ: Lawrence Erlbaum Associates, 1988).

Velody, I. and Williams, R. 'Introduction', in I. Velody and R. Williams (eds) *The Politics of Constructionism* (London: Sage, 1998), pp. 1–12.

Victor, J.S. 'A Rumor-panic About a Dangerous Satanic Cult in Western New York', *New York Folklore*, XV:1–2 (1989), 23–49.

Victor, J. S. *Satanic Panic: The Creation of a Contemporary Legend* (Chicago: Open Court, 1993).

Wayne, M. *Marxism and Media Studies: Key Concepts and Contemporary Trends* (London: Pluto Press, 2003).

Weatherall, A. *Gender, Language and Discourse* (London: Routledge, 2002).

Weber, M. *Economy and Society: An Outline of Interpretive Sociology* (Berkeley: University of California Press, 1978). Originally published in 1920 as *Wirtschaft und Gesellschaft*.

Weber, M. *The Protestant Ethic and the Spirit of Capitalism* (London: Routledge, 2001). Originally published in 1905 as *Die protestantische Ethik und der Geist des Kapitalismus*.

Weinberg, D. 'The Philosophical Foundations of Constructionist Research', in J.A.

Holstein and J.F. Gubrium (eds) *Handbook of Constructionist Research* (New York: The Guilford Press, 2008), pp. 13–39.

White, P. *Developing Research Questions: A Guide for Social Scientists* (Basingstoke: Palgrave, 2009).

Williams, R.H. 'Constructing the Public Good: Social Movements and Cultural Resources' *Social Problems* 42:1 (1995), 124–144.

Willig, C. 'Social Constructionism and Revolutionary Socialism: A Contradiction in Terms', in Ian Parker (ed.) *Social Constructionism, Realism and Discourse* (London: Sage, 1998), pp. 91–104.

Willis, P.E. *Profane Culture* (London: Routledge and Kegan Paul, 1978).

Willis, P.E. *Learning to Labour: How Working Class Kids get Working Class Jobs* (Westmead: Saxon House, 1979).

Woolgar, S. and Pawluch, D. 'Ontological Gerrymandering: The Anatomy of Social Problems Explanations' *Social Problems* 32:3 (1985a), 214–27.

Woolgar, S. and Pawluch, D. 'How Shall We Move Beyond Constructivism?' *Social Problems* 33:2 (1985b), 159–62.

Wuthnow, R. 'Religion as a Sacred Canopy', in James Davison Hunter and Stephen C. Ainlay (eds) *Making Sense of Modern Times: Peter L. Berger and the Vision of Interpretive Sociology* (London and New York: Routledge and Kegan Paul, 1986), pp. 121–142.

Wuthnow, R. *After Heaven: Spirituality in America since the 1950s* (Princeton, NJ: Princeton University Press, 1998).

Zatz, M. S. 'Chicano Youth Gangs and Crime: The Creation of a Moral Panic', *Contemporary Crises* 11:2 (1987), 129–58.

Index

Abercrombie, N.   31
agency   19, 82–4, 89, 90, 96, 97–100,
   102–106, 111
Alcoholics Anonymous   30
alienation   31–2
Amnesty International   50
anomy (anomie)   31
Ashmore, M.   91

Ben-Yehuda, N.   45–8
Berger, P.L.   7, 8, 17–36, 58, 59, 62,
   72, 74, 81, 96, 97, 99, 101–103,
   110
Best, J.   96, 97, 104
biology   3, 13, 15, 22, 23, 66–8, 100
Burr, V.   100
Butler, J.   67, 98

capitalism   34, 79, 84–6
Carrie   9
Catholicism *see* Christianity
CDA *see* critical discourse analysis
Chicago School, The   37
Christianity   10, 11, 15, 24, 29, 32–5,
   42, 45, 63
   Catholic   30, 35
   Protestant   34–5
Civil Rights Movement   51, 111
claims   40–49, 51, 54, 90, 91, 99,
   111–12
   definition of   41
claims-making   40–49, 54, 56, 90, 96,
   104, 111, 112
   primary   44–5
   secondary   44–5
cognition   6, 59–61, 68–69
cognitive psychology *see* psychology
collective representations   19
common sense   2, 17, 18, 22, 32, 48,
   53, 62, 66, 74, 76–77

constructivism   3, 7, 103
context   14, 48, 52, 53, 61, 72, 77, 80,
   82, 84, 85, 109–10
contextual constructionism *see* realism
contingency   3–4, 15, 100
convention   2–3, 21
crime   37, 39, 42, 45, 47, 50, 52–6
   concern over   53–4
   effects of crime images   54–6
criminology   47
   news-making   47, 111
critical realism   72, 87, 105
critical discourse analysis   7, 8, 71–80,
   82, 85, 86, 95, 102, 103, 104,
   105, 112
Crotty, M.   91, 93, 107, 108

definition of the situation   10, 15
Derrida, J.   63
Desecularization of the World, The   36
deviance   39, 47–8, 56, 59
   secondary deviation   55
dialectics   19, 22, 23, 32, 34, 35, 36,
   77, 78, 86, 97, 105
dialogue   12, 64, 94
differentiation   33, 34, 63, 65, 67
discourse   5–6, 15, 26, 58–64, 67–8,
   71–80, 90–97, 106
   action orientation   6, 60
   definition of   5–6
   discourse in the world position   88,
      89, 93–7, 104
   political   76
   world in discourse position   88,
      90–93, 98, 99, 102, 104, 109, 110
discourse analysis   5, 58–9, 108
   critical *see* Critical Discourse Analysis
   textually-oriented   84
discourse in the world *see* discourse
Division of Labour in Society, The   48